QUICK COURSE®

in Creating a Web Site Using

MICROSOFT FrontPage 2000

Fast-track training® for busy people

BOOK SALE

JOYCE COX

CHRISTINA DUDLEY

PUBLISHED BY
Online Press
15442 Bel-Red Road
Redmond, WA 98052
Phone: (425) 885-1441, (800) 854-3344
Fax: (425) 881-1642
E-mail: quickcourse@otsiweb.com
Web site: www.quickcourse.com

Copyright © 1999 by Online Press

Online Press is an imprint of Online Training Solutions, Inc.

All rights reserved. No part of the contents of this book may be reproduced or transmitted in any form or by any means without the written permission of the publisher.

Publisher's Cataloging-in-Publication
(Provided by Quality Books, Inc.)

Cox, Joyce.
    Quick Course in creating a web site using
Microsoft FrontPage 2000 / Joyce Cox, Christina
Dudley. -- 1st ed.
    p. cm. -- (Quick Course books)
    Includes index.
    ISBN: 1-58278-008-0

    1. Microsoft FrontPage.   2. Web sites--Design.
I. Dudley, Christina. II. Title. III. Title:
Creating a web site using Microsoft FrontPage 2000
IV. Series.

    TK5105.8885.F76C69 1999   005.7'2
                          QBI99-500171
                                       99-070322
                                             CIP

Printed and bound in the United States of America.

1 2 3 4 5 6 7 8 9 B P B P 3 2 1 0

Fast-Track Training®, Online Press®, and Quick Course® are registered trademarks of Online Press Inc. FrontPage, Microsoft, Microsoft Press, PowerPoint, Windows, and Windows NT are either registered trademarks or trademarks of Microsoft Corporation in the United States and/or other countries. Other product and company names mentioned herein may be the trademarks of their respective owners.

The example companies, organizations, products, people, and events depicted herein are fictitious. No association with any real company, organization, product, person, or event is intended or should be inferred.

Content overview

Introduction ix

PART ONE: LEARNING THE BASICS

1 Creating a Simple Web Site 2

We introduce you to FrontPage, Microsoft's Web authoring program. Using a FrontPage wizard, you create a simple set of Web pages. In the process, you learn how to reorganize pages, add and edit text, get help, and quit the program.

2 Enhancing Your Web 32

First you add graphics and a theme to your web to give its pages some pizazz. Next you create various types of hyperlinks and bookmarks. Finally, you learn how to add navigation bars.

3 Publishing Your Web Site 56

You prepare your Web site for publication by spell-checking pages, verifying and editing hyperlinks, and previewing the web in a Web browser and on paper. We then discuss how to find a Web server and how to send the web to the server.

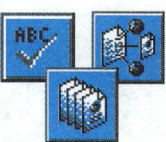

PART TWO: BUILDING PROFICIENCY

4 Creating a More Complex Web 76

In this chapter, you take a look at some of the more complex elements you can add to a web. First you create a new web so that you can experiment with a frames page. Next you insert and format a table. Finally, you work with forms.

5 Adding Special Effects 106

In this chapter, you learn how to add special effects. You look at more advanced graphics techniques, including hotspots. You add hover buttons, marquees, and hit counters. You also insert sound, video, and non-HTML components.

6 Maintaining and Updating a Web 132

You first work with the tasks list, which you use to keep track of your web's pages. Next you see how to use comments and keep your site up-to-date with included pages, scheduled pages, and variables. Then you update a published web.

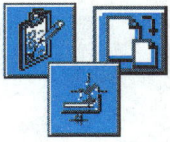

Index 154

Content details

Introduction ix

PART ONE: LEARNING THE BASICS

1 Creating a Simple Web Site 2
Getting Started 5
FrontPage Concepts 10
Creating a Web 10
    Deciding What Information You Need 11
    Using a Wizard 11
Reorganizing a Web 15
    Deleting Pages 17
    Adding Pages 18
Working in Page View 20
    Adding and Editing Text 21
    Using the Page View Tabs 23
    Formatting Text 24
        Changing Paragraph Alignment 26
        Controlling Paragraph Spacing 26
        Creating Numbered and Bulleted Lists 26
Renaming Files 28
Getting Help 29
Quitting FrontPage 31

2 Enhancing Your Web 32
Adding Graphics to a Web 34
    Sizing and Positioning Graphics 36
    Searching for Graphics 39
        Searching for Graphics on the Web 40
Applying a Different Theme 41
Adding Hyperlinks 43
    Linking to a New Page 44
    Linking to an Existing Page 46
    Adding E-mail Hyperlinks 47
    Adding Links to Other Web Sites 48
    Adding Links to Bookmarks 50
Working with Navigation Bars 51

3 Publishing Your Web Site   56

Preparing Your Web for Publishing 58
   Checking Spelling..58
      Checking the Spelling of an Entire Page 59
      Checking the Spelling of Multiple Pages 60
   Checking Hyperlinks 62
      Checking in Hyperlinks View.....................................62
      Checking in Reports View 63
      Editing Hyperlinks 65
   Previewing a Web 66
   Printing a Web 68
Publishing a Web 69
   About FrontPage Server Extensions 69
   Finding a Web Presence Provider 70
   Sending a Web to a Server 71
Deleting a FrontPage Web 72

PART TWO: BUILDING PROFICIENCY

4 Creating a More Complex Web   76

Creating a Web from Scratch..78
   Making Design Decisions 78
      Defining the Target Audience....................................79
      Defining the Content..79
   Starting an Empty Web..80
Creating a Frames Page 82
   Using a Frames Page Template......................................83
   Setting Up the Contents Frame 84
   Setting Up the Main Frame 86
   Refining a Frames Page 87
Creating Tables 89
   Rearranging a Table 92
   Adding a Title 92
   Formatting a Table 93
Creating Visitor Input Forms 95
   Customizing a Placeholder Form..................................95
   Modifying Field Properties 98
   Previewing an Input Form 101
   Collecting Data from an Input Form..........................103

5 Adding Special Effects — 106

- More About Graphics 108
  - Formatting a Graphic 108
  - Using Hotspots 111
- Working with Animated Objects 114
  - Adding DHTML Effects 114
  - Creating a Hover Button 116
  - Creating a Marquee 118
  - Adding a Hit Counter 120
  - Using Sound Effects 122
  - Adding Video 124
- Working with Non-HTML Components 126
  - Adding ActiveX Controls 127
  - Adding Java Applets 129

6 Maintaining and Updating a Web — 132

- Using the Tasks List 134
  - Creating Tasks 135
  - Editing Tasks 137
  - Working on Tasks 138
- Keeping a Web Site Up-to-Date 141
  - Documenting a Web with Comments 141
  - Using an Include Page 143
    - Changing an Include Page 145
    - Using a Scheduled Include Page 145
  - Working with Variables 147
- Publishing New Web Pages 150

Introduction

If you want to learn how to create a Web site, you probably already know enough about the Internet and the World Wide Web to be able to skip this introduction. But for those of you who'd like a basic orientation before you get started, we'll toss out a few definitions to set the scene.

- **The Internet.** A contraction of *inter-networks* (or *between networks*). Started in the '60s as a connection between Department of Defense computers at four sites across the US, the Internet now connects millions of computers all over the world. Nobody "owns" the Internet, and nobody has overall management responsibility.

- **The World Wide Web.** Invented by Tim Berners-Lee in 1989. The Web, as it is called, is part of the Internet. Like the Internet, it's not a *thing*. Unlike the Internet, the Web is governed by a tight set of rules that specify how text, graphics, and other information should be coded so that information on one computer can be linked to information on another computer in a potentially infinite "web." The rules also mean that Web information is consistent, making access to it easier for beginning and intermediate Internet users.

- **HyperText Markup Language (HTML).** The coding system that controls how Web information is interpreted and displayed. HTML is the standard for all Web documents. It relies on a set of beginning and ending codes, or *tags*, that enclose each element. In the days when Web sites were relatively simple, these tags were often manually inserted. But as the complexity of Web sites has increased, it has become easier to use a Web authoring program like Microsoft FrontPage 2000 to handle the HTML coding, allowing you to focus on the site's content.

- **Web sites.** Information resources published on the Web by government agencies, companies, organizations, and individuals. Each site has an address, called a *Universal Resource Locator* (*URL*), that identifies the computer on which the files that make up the site's information are stored. These files can consist of text, graphics, and multimedia components such as audio and video clips.

- **Web pages.** The chunks of linked information that comprise a Web site. The starting point of each site is its *home page*. You can jump from one page to another both within a Web site and between sites by clicking *hyperlinks*, pointers that appear on the screen as specially formatted text or as graphics, but that include HTML codes specifying the address of the link's target.

- **Web servers.** Computers on which special software has been installed to both manage the files that comprise a Web site and make those files available for viewing. Web servers can be single computers that are visited only by the employees of a particular company, or banks of computers that are visited by millions of people. Server capacity and the volume of traffic combine to determine how fast the Web pages on a particular server can be downloaded and viewed.

- **Web browsers.** Programs you run on your computer so that you can view information stored on a Web server. The browser interprets the HTML coding, displays the information on your screen, and enables you to move between linked items.

- **Intranets.** Private Web look-alikes. Using Internet technology, many companies are setting up Web servers and creating Web sites that are accessible only from the company's computers. Intranets enable people to easily and cheaply access company information, exchange ideas, and collaborate on projects.

That's it for the definitions for now. With that common understanding of what you're working with, let's turn our attention to FrontPage 2000.

PART ONE

LEARNING THE BASICS

In Part One, we cover basic techniques for working with Microsoft FrontPage 2000. After you complete these three chapters, you'll know enough to be able to create and publish simple, yet effective Web pages. In Chapter 1, you learn how to work with the program while creating Web pages using one of FrontPage's built-in wizards. In Chapter 2, you enhance the look of your pages by adding graphics and a theme, and you create hyperlinks and bookmarks. In Chapter 3, you prepare your pages for publication on the World Wide Web or on an intranet.

1
Creating a Simple Web Site

In this chapter, we introduce you to FrontPage, Microsoft's Web-authoring program. Using one of the program's wizards, you create a simple set of web pages. In the process, you learn how to reorganize pages, add and edit text, get help, and quit the program.

Our example is for a company that organizes cycling tours, but you can use FrontPage to create pages for your community or campus organization, your company's intranet, or even for yourself.

Web pages created and concepts covered:

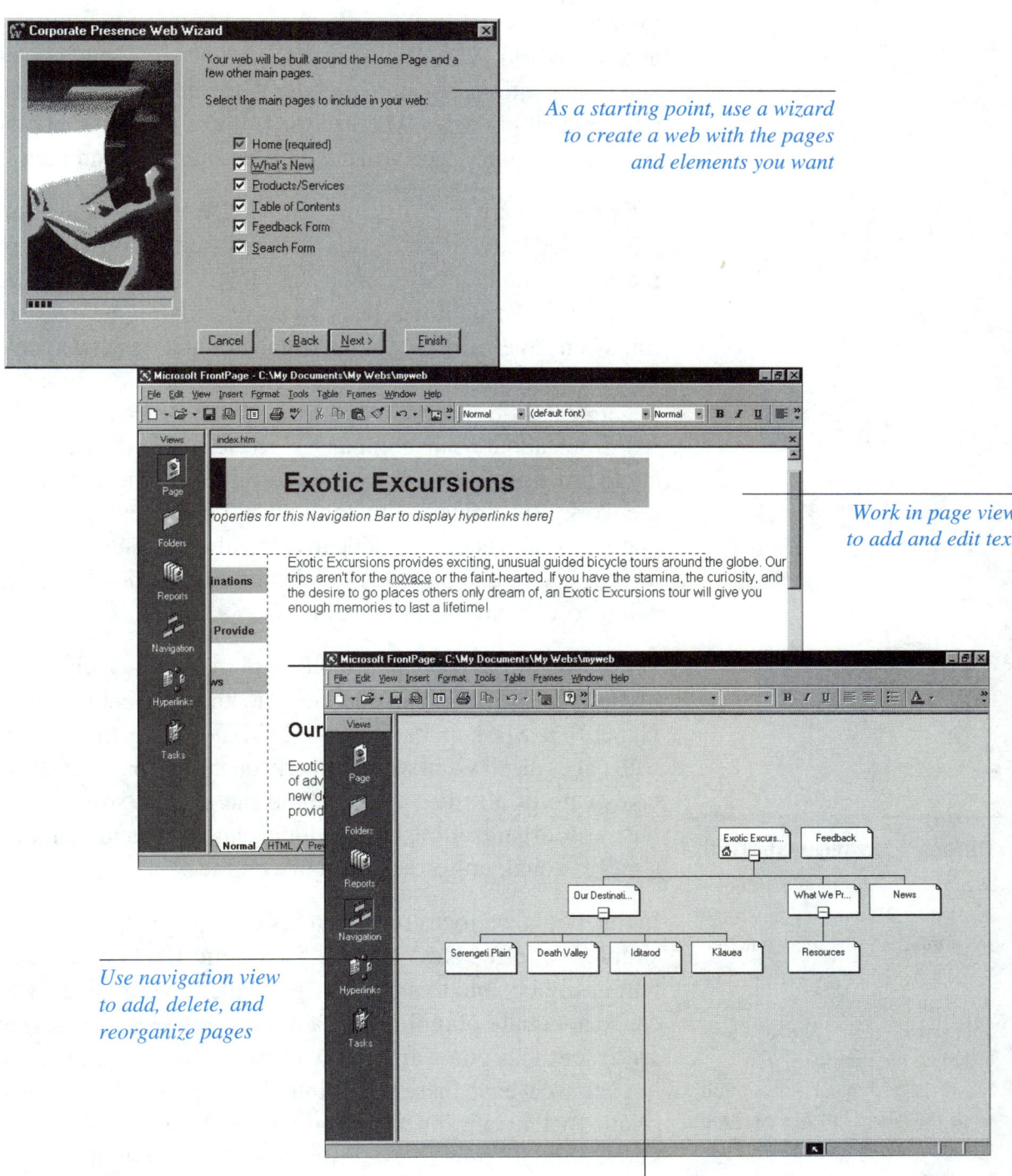

As a starting point, use a wizard to create a web with the pages and elements you want

Work in page view to add and edit text

Use navigation view to add, delete, and reorganize pages

Change a page title in this view and it is automatically updated throughout the web

Before the Internet and the World Wide Web became accessible to the general public, businesses and organizations relied on printed publications to promote their products and services. As the popularity of the Internet and the World Wide Web grew, the more savvy businesses and organizations began to include Web sites in their overall promotional strategies. These days, it almost goes without saying that an organization will have a Web site on the Internet.

Suppose you are in charge of creating a Web site for a company called Exotic Excursions that organizes bicycle tours of the more remote areas around the globe. We're not talking about meandering down leafy lanes or pedaling paved bike trails here. We're talking about rough, tough rides that appeal to hard-core, thrill-seeking cyclists. How are you going to generate a Web site that will attract this audience and get the word out about your company's services? Obviously, you could hire a professional designer to guide you and do most of the work. But suppose you don't have the budget to take this approach. You need to be able to create the Web site yourself. That's where a sophisticated Web-authoring program like Microsoft FrontPage 2000 comes in.

With FrontPage, you can produce and manage a Web site in just a few easy steps. You don't need to know the cumbersome HyperText Markup Language (HTML) coding that makes web pages display and work properly on the screen. FrontPage takes care of all the coding behind the scenes, so now any business, organization, or individual can create and maintain a professional, up-to-date presence on the Web.

In this book, we focus on how to use FrontPage to produce a simple, yet effective Web site for Exotic Excursions. You will easily be able to adapt this example to your needs. Because adequate planning and a basic knowledge of design are essential if you want your web pages to have maximum impact, we weave these topics into the chapters where appropriate. By the time you have worked through this book, you'll know not only how to use FrontPage, but how to develop a variety of web pages that accomplish your goals.

Different configurations

We are using a computer running Microsoft Windows 98 with a resolution of 800x600 and the taskbar hidden. If you are using a different version or resolution, your screen might not match ours exactly. Our FrontPage configuration is a Typical installation from the Microsoft Office 2000 CD-ROM. If your setup is different, don't worry; you will still be able to follow along with most of the examples in this book.

We assume that you have already installed both Microsoft Windows 95 or a later version and Microsoft FrontPage 2000 on your computer. We also assume that you've worked with Windows before and that you know how to start programs, move windows, choose commands from menus, select text, and so on. If you are a new Windows user, we suggest you take a look at the *Quick Course® in Microsoft® Windows®* book that is appropriate for your operating system so that you can quickly come up to speed.

Getting Started

Before you start work, let's quickly take a look at FrontPage. We'll show you what the program window looks like and how to give instructions. Here we go:

1. Click the Start button and choose Programs and then Microsoft FrontPage from the Start menu.

Starting FrontPage

2. If FrontPage displays a dialog box asking whether you want it to be your default web page editor, click Yes.

3. If FrontPage needs to determine your computer's settings, click OK. Click OK again when the settings have been determined. Your screen then looks as shown here:

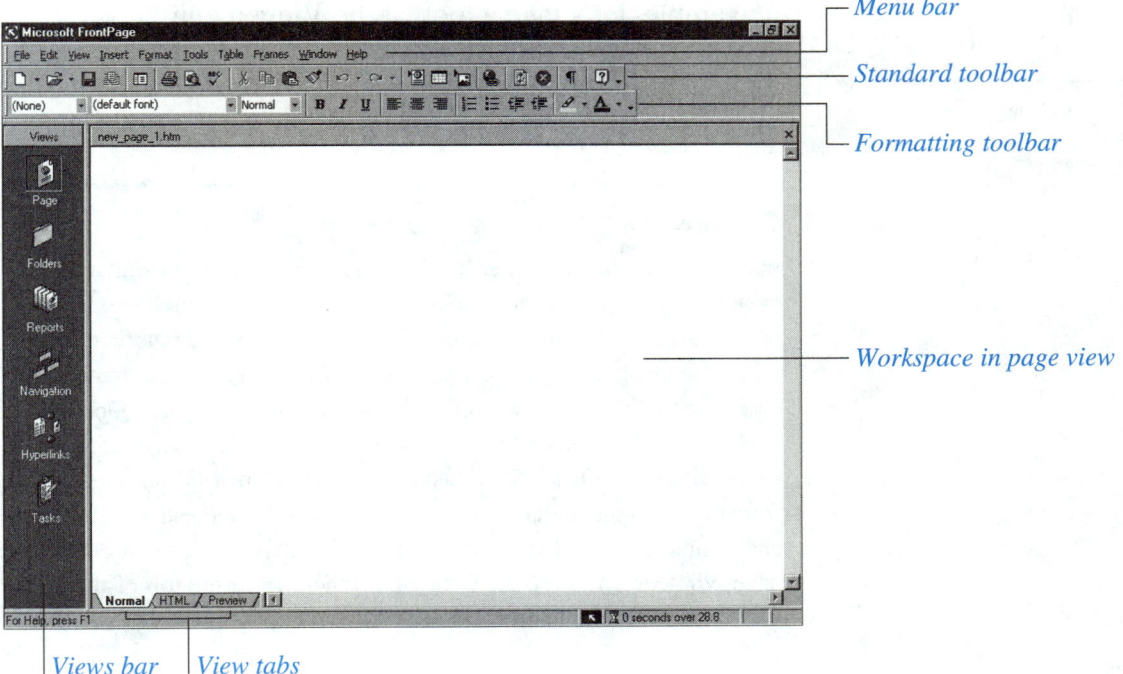

Like most Windows applications, the FrontPage window includes the familiar title bar at the top and a status bar at the bottom. You also see a menu bar, a Views bar, and toolbars, which you use to give FrontPage instructions. You may not have worked with an element like the Views bar before, and although the menu bar and toolbars look the same as those in all Windows applications, they work a little differently, so we'll take a moment to explore them here.

The Views bar

The Page icon

The *Views bar* is an area to the left of the workspace that contains a set of icons that you click to change your view of your work. At the moment, you are looking at an empty workspace in page view. (If your screen looks different from the one on the previous page, click the Page icon on the Views bar to switch to page view.) You'll work in the other views as you follow along with the examples in this book.

The menu bar, menus, and commands

The *menu bar* consists of *menus* that organize the *commands* available for the component you are working with. You use standard Windows techniques to choose a command from a menu or submenu and to work with dialog boxes. However, FrontPage 2000 goes beyond the basic Windows procedure for choosing commands by determining which commands you are most likely to use and adjusting the display of commands on each menu to reflect how you use the program. As an example, let's take a look at the View menu:

Short menus

1. Click *View* on the menu bar to drop down the View menu. The two arrows at the bottom of the menu indicate that one or

> **Other ways to start FrontPage**
>
> Instead of starting FrontPage by choosing it from the Start menu, you can create a FrontPage shortcut icon on your desktop. Right-click an open area of the desktop and choose New and then Shortcut from the shortcut menu. In the Create Shortcut dialog box, click the Browse button, navigate to the C:\Program Files\Microsoft Office\Office\frontpg file, click Open, and click Next. Type a name for the shortcut icon and click Finish. If you are using Microsoft Office 2000, you can choose Open Office Document from the top of the Start menu, navigate to the web page you want to open, and double-click its filename. To start FrontPage and open a new web page, you can choose New Office Document from the top of the Start menu and then double-click the Web Page icon.

more commands are hidden because they are not the ones most people use most of the time.

2. Continue pointing to the word *View*. The two arrows disappear, and the menu expands like this to show more commands:

Expanded menus

(You can also click the two arrows to make hidden commands appear.) The status of a less frequently used command is indicated by a lighter shade of gray. If you choose one of the light gray commands, in the future it will appear in the same color as other commands and will no longer be hidden.

3. Choose the Reveal Tags command. In the workspace, FrontPage displays the underlying HTML tags that begin and end every web page, like this:

Turning HTML tags on/off

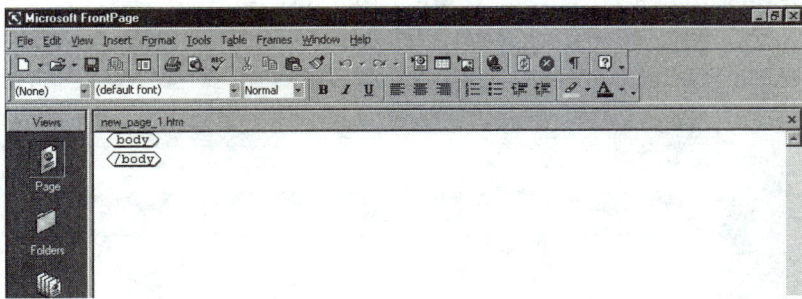

You won't work directly with HTML code as you work your way through this book. However, by taking a look at the coding behind your pages from time to time, you might be inspired to learn more about it. If so, check the HTML topic in FrontPage's Help feature (see page 29).

4. Click the View menu, notice that the Reveal Tags command now appears on the menu, and choose it to turn off the tags.

Shortcut menus

The commands you can use with a particular object, such as text or a toolbar, are grouped on special menus called *shortcut menus*. You display an object's shortcut menu by pointing to the object and clicking the right mouse button. (This action is called *right-clicking*.) In this book, we choose shortcut menu commands when that is the most efficient way to accomplish a task.

Toolbars

Another way to give FrontPage an instruction is by clicking a button on a *toolbar*. This is the equivalent of choosing the corresponding command from a menu and if necessary, clicking OK to accept all the default settings in the command's dialog box. FrontPage arranges its most frequently used buttons on two toolbars, the Standard and Formatting toolbars, above the workspace. Other toolbars are available but hidden so that they don't take up screen space unless you need them. As shown here, each toolbar has a *move handle* at its left end, which you can drag to move the toolbar on the screen:

Move handles

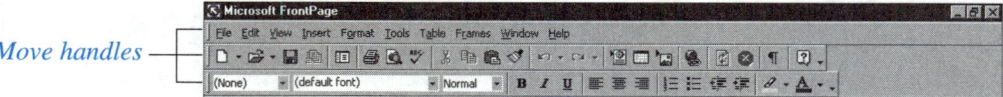

Move handles

As you can see, the menu bar has a move handle, too. In practice, you don't usually move the menu bar as much as the toolbars. Let's do some exploring:

1. Point to each toolbar button, pausing until its name appears in a box below the pointer. This feature is called *ScreenTips*.

ScreenTips

2. Point to the Formatting toolbar's move handle, and when the pointer changes to a four-headed arrow, hold down the mouse button and drag the toolbar down over the workspace, where it becomes a "floating" toolbar like this one:

Floating toolbars

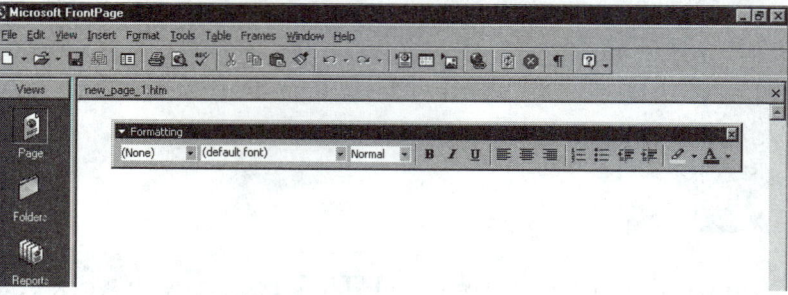

Docking toolbars

3. Double-click the toolbar's title bar to "dock" it at the top of the workspace again. You can dock a toolbar along any side of the program window simply by dragging it there. (Drag a docked toolbar by its move handle or a floating toolbar by its title bar.) As you have seen, when you double-click the floating toolbar's title bar to redock it, the toolbar automatically returns to its previous docked location.

4. Now drag the Formatting toolbar's move handle up over the Standard toolbar. FrontPage overlaps the two toolbars on a single toolbar row below the menu bar. When part of a toolbar is hidden, FrontPage displays the toolbar's most frequently used buttons.

One toolbar row

5. Suppose you want to see fewer of the Formatting toolbar's buttons and more of the Standard toolbar's buttons. Drag the Formatting toolbar's move handle to the right until it sits under the Help menu. As shown here, each toolbar now has a More Buttons button at its right end, which you can click to display a palette of the hidden buttons:

Displaying more/fewer buttons

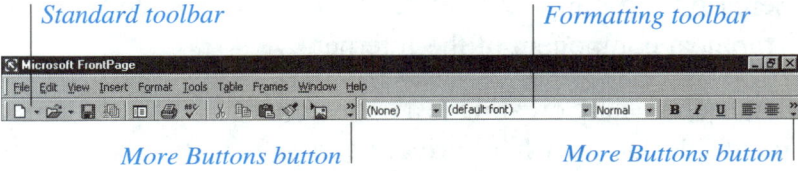

6. Click the Standard toolbar's More Buttons button to see this palette of all the hidden buttons on that toolbar:

The More Buttons button

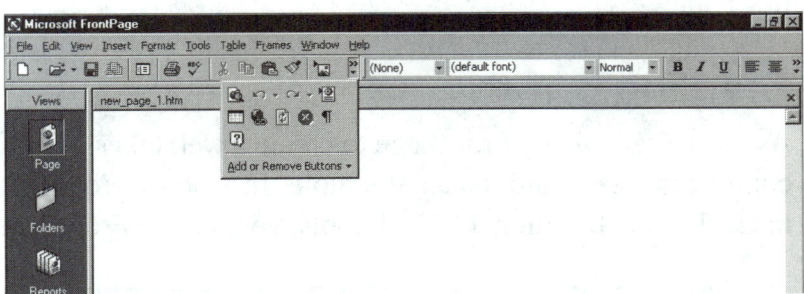

If you click a button on this palette, FrontPage adjusts the relative size of the toolbars to make room for it.

Personalized menus and toolbars

FrontPage's menus and toolbars adjust themselves to the way that you work, making more commands and buttons available as you use them. Commands and buttons you don't use are hidden so that they don't get in the way. As a result, your menus and toolbars may not look exactly like ours, and occasionally, we may tell you to choose a command or click a button that is not visible. When this happens, don't panic. Simply pull down the menu and wait for all its commands to be displayed, or click the toolbar's More Buttons button to display its hidden buttons. If you want to restore your menus and toolbars to their original settings, choose Toolbars and then Customize from the View menu and on the Options tab, click Reset My Usage Data, and then click OK.

7. Click a blank area of the workspace to close the palette.

With that brief introduction to the menu bar and toolbars out of the way, let's briefly go over some basic FrontPage concepts.

FrontPage Concepts

→ **A web**
→ **A Web Site**

In FrontPage terminology, a *web* is a set of *pages* that you are creating on your computer. It does not become a full-fledged *Web site* until it is stored on a Web server and is accessible for viewing by other people. In this book, we follow FrontPage's lead and refer to the pages you are in the process of creating as a *web* (with a lowercase *w*). We use the term *Web* (with an uppercase *W*) for anything related to the World Wide Web, the graphical component of the Internet.

→ **Hyperlinks**

The web you are creating is a collection of files that is stored in a folder on your hard drive. Each page is its own file and can include text, graphics, and other elements. The web's pages are usually linked together by *hyperlinks*, and they may also be linked to other Web sites. (We discuss hyperlinks in Chapter 2.)

Creating a Web

As we've said, using FrontPage to create a web takes a fairly complicated task and makes it simple. Instead of producing the web using traditional HTML tools, you rely on FrontPage

> **Web design considerations**
>
> If you have a lot of information to share with visitors to your web, you will want to split the information between related pages. By carefully planning the structure of your web, you can direct how visitors interact with your site, as well as the information you present. If you want to place pictures, graphics, or other images on your pages, be aware of the time it takes for a browser to download those images to a viewer's computer screen. (You can check the estimated download time of a particular page by displaying the page and looking at the time displayed in the status bar.) Your goal should be to give your viewers all the information you want to provide without overwhelming them with excessive reading or creating a page that loads so slowly that viewers give up and move elsewhere. Smaller pages load faster, so you will want to limit the size of pages that contain graphics, sound files, or other memory-intensive features.

to add the HTML codes that Web browsers need to be able to display the web pages on viewer's screens. All you have to do is make decisions about what you want on the pages and how you want each item to look and operate.

Deciding What Information You Need

Deciding what should appear on each page is the most important step in producing a web, and is also the most overlooked. Most people are too eager to jump right in and get going, but planning is crucial in developing your presence on an intranet or the Internet. You don't have to make every decision ahead of time. With FrontPage, it's easy to make changes both during the initial creation process and afterward. But you should have a solid idea of what information you want to share and how you want to link items. Planning methods include drawing a flowchart on paper, using file cards (each with a notation that represents a page), or actually storyboarding the web. We talk more about this planning phase on page 79.

Using a Wizard

After the planning phase, the simplest way to create a web is to use one of FrontPage's built-in wizards. So let's get started:

1. Click the arrow to the right of the New Page button on the Standard toolbar and select Web from the drop-down list to display this dialog box:

The New Page button

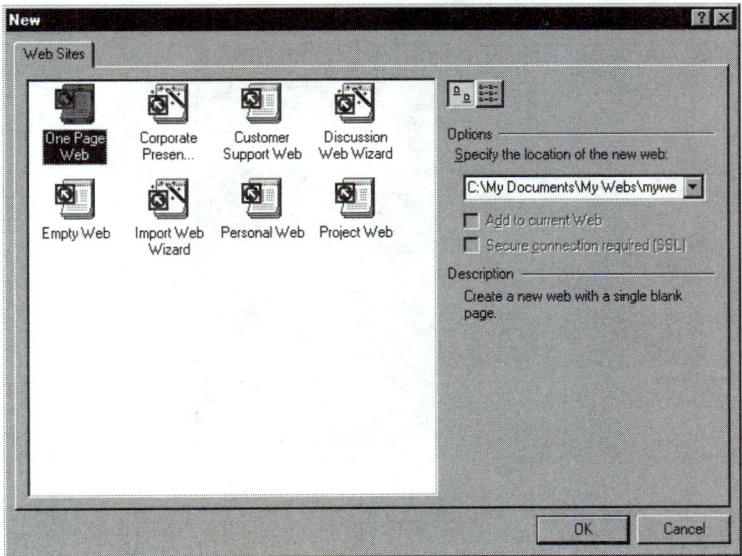

The Corporate Presence Wizard

2. Click the Corporate Presence Wizard icon, check that C:\My Documents\My Webs\myweb is displayed in the Specify The Location Of The New Web edit box, and click OK. (Myweb is the name of the folder FrontPage will create to store all the components of your new web.)

FrontPage opens the folder list in a pane to the left of the workspace and displays the first dialog box of the Corporate Presence Web Wizard. Follow these steps to set up your web's pages:

1. Read the information in the dialog box and then click Next to display this dialog box:

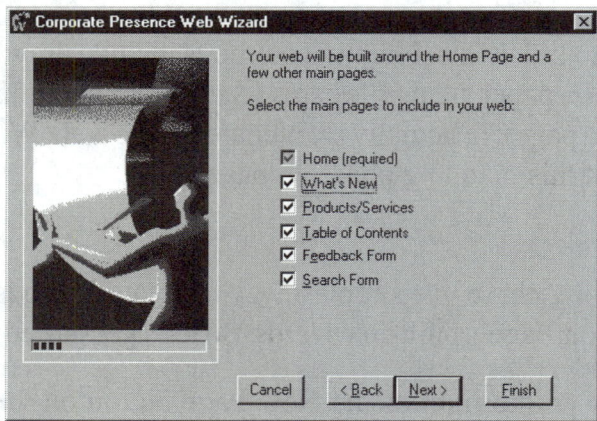

2. Deselect the Table Of Contents and Search Form check boxes and then click Next to display this dialog box:

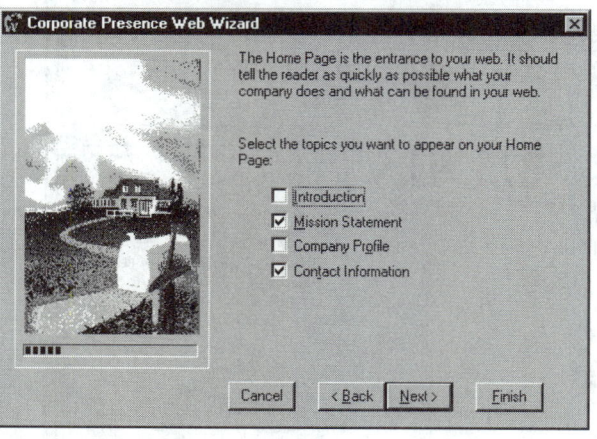

3. Click the Introduction and Company Profile check boxes so that all the check boxes are selected. Then click Next.

Other ways to create a new web

The New dialog box provides several wizards and templates for creating a new web. You can create one-page webs and empty (blank) webs, as well as webs for customer support, discussions, personal information, or projects. You can also use the Import Web Wizard to import a web that you have already created in another program.

4. In the next dialog box, deselect Web Changes and click the Articles And Reviews check box to designate what will appear on the What's New page. Then click Next.

5. Enter *0* in the Products box, enter *5* in the Services box, and click Next.

6. Check that Information Request Form is the only check box selected and click Next to see the dialog box shown here:

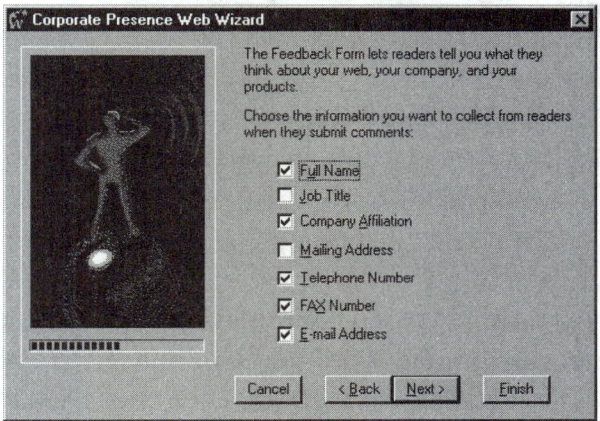

7. Click all the check boxes so you can collect as much information as possible about your visitors and then click Next.

8. You do not want your feedback file to use a tab-delimited format, so click No and then Next to display this dialog box:

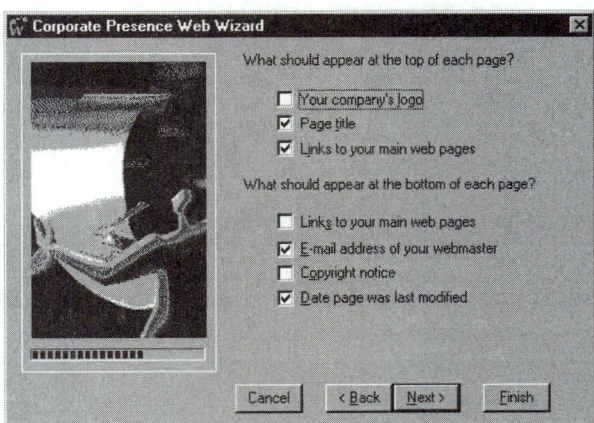

9. Check that Page Title and Links To Your Main Web Pages are selected for the top and E-mail Address Of Your Webmaster

Tab-delimited format

If you want to be able to merge the information you receive from the Feedback Form page into a database or spreadsheet program for analysis, click Yes when asked whether the feedback file should use a tab-delimited format. That way, the items of information will be separated by tabs and can easily be interpreted into records and fields.

and Date Page Was Last Modified are selected for the bottom of each page. Then click Next.

10. Click No to skip using an Under Construction icon, and then click Next to display this dialog box:

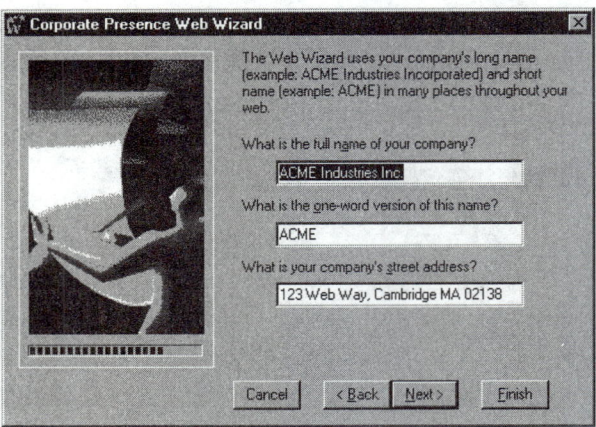

11. Type *Exotic Excursions* as the full name of the company, type *Exotic-Excursions* as the one-word version, and *123 Park Place, Bellevue, WA 98007* as the address. Then click Next to display this dialog box:

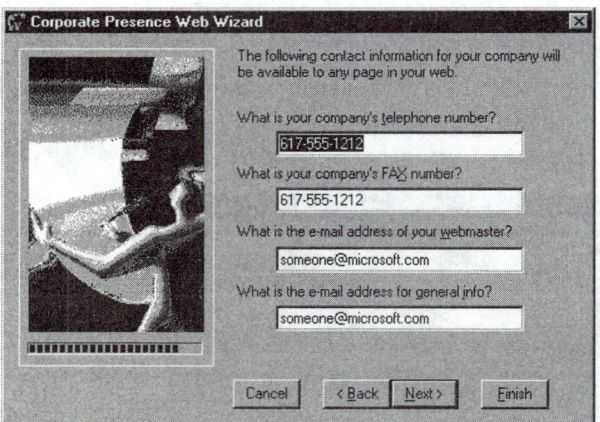

12. Enter the information shown below in the appropriate edit boxes and then click Next:

Phone number	*425-555-1212*
Fax number	*425-555-1213*
Webmaster e-mail address	*wendyw@exoticexcursions.tld*
General e-mail address	*info@exoticexcursions.tld*

13. For now, you want to keep your web simple, so click Next to apply the default Corporate Presence theme to your web. (You'll apply a different theme in Chapter 2.)

14. Click Finish in the wizard's last dialog box. The wizard closes, and FrontPage switches to tasks view, as shown here:

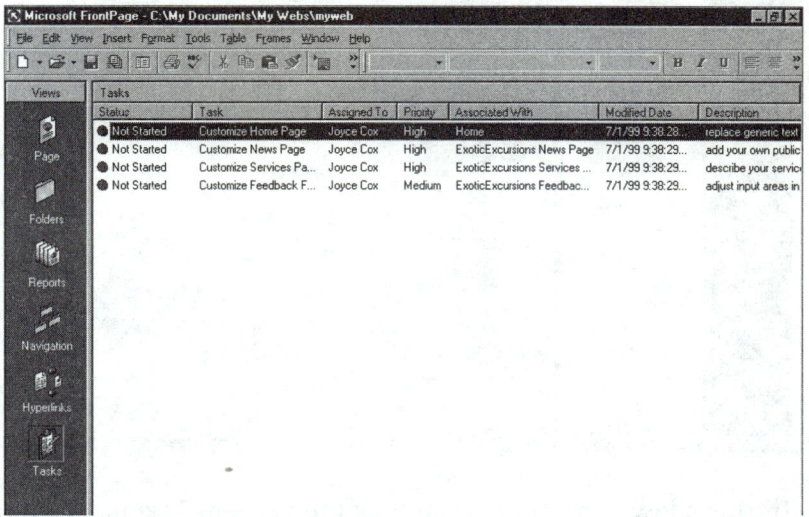

In this view, you can take a look at each page of your web and check items such as its status and priority. If you want to work on a particular page, you can select the page in tasks view, right-click it, and choose either Start Task or Edit Task from the shortcut menu (see the tip on page 7). You can also mark tasks as complete, or you can delete them. To return to this view at any time, simply click the Tasks icon on the Views bar. Before you begin entering information in your pages, though, you need to do a little reorganizing.

The Tasks icon

Reorganizing a Web

Using a FrontPage wizard makes the creation of a web much easier, but unfortunately, the wizards don't always organize your web exactly the way you want it. After setting up a web using a wizard, you will probably want to look over its structure and make some adjustments by moving, adding, or deleting some pages. The best way to complete this sort of reorganization is by looking at the web in navigation view. Follow the steps on the next page.

Initial capital letters

Sometimes the capitalization of the option names we use doesn't exactly match what's on the screen. We capitalize the first letter of every word to set these words off in a sentence. For example, on page 13 we tell you to select the Date Page Was Last Modified option when the option name on the screen is Date page was last modified.

The Navigation icon

1. Click the Navigation icon on the Views bar to display your web as shown here:

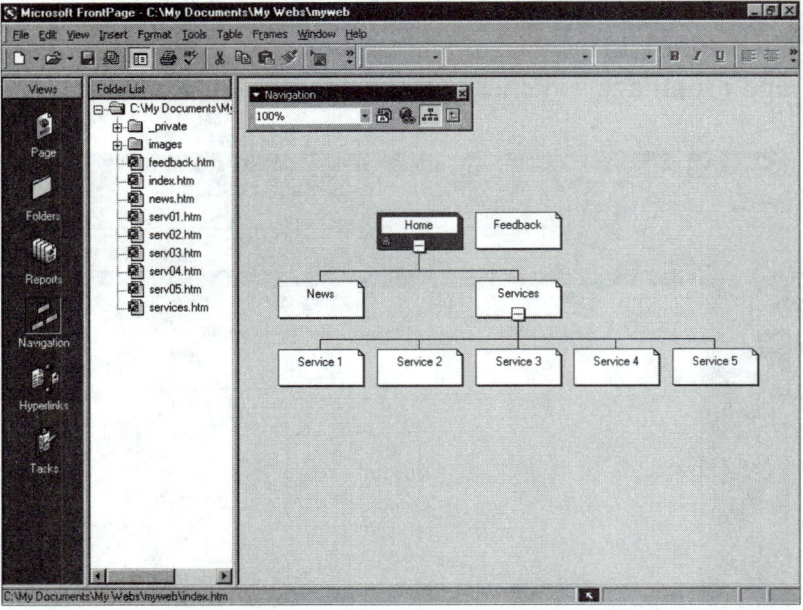

In this view, FrontPage displays the present layout of your web in a familiar flowchart format. It also turns on the Navigation toolbar (we've moved it out of the way) and opens the folder list, which displays your web's folders and files, to the left of the workspace. (The folder list can be viewed in its own window by clicking the Folders icon on the Views bar.) Each of the boxes in the workspace represents a page of your web. The *home page* is identified by the small icon in the bottom left corner of the Home box. A plus icon (+) on a box indicates that this *parent page* contains hidden *child pages*. You can display the child pages by clicking the plus icon. When the child pages are visible, the plus icon changes to a minus icon (–), and clicking the minus icon closes the child pages, giving you a more compact view of your web. You can move any of the boxes using standard drag-and-drop methods.

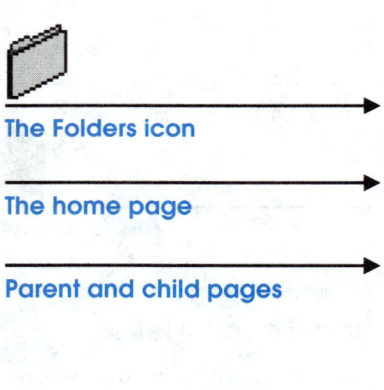

The Folders icon

The home page

Parent and child pages

2. To view more of the navigation pane, click the Folder List button on the Standard toolbar to toggle it off. Then click the Close button on the Navigation toolbar to turn it off.

The Folder List button

3. Click the minus icon on the Services box to collapse its five child pages, as shown on the facing page.

Collapsing the structure

Chapter 1 Creating a Simple Web Site   17

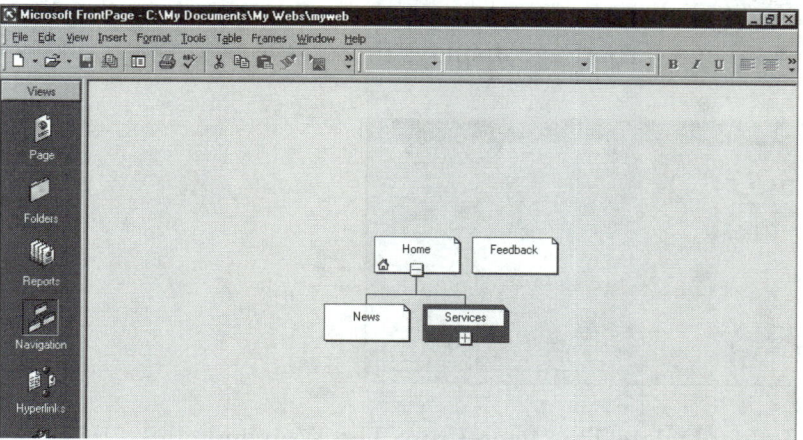

4. Click the minus icon on the Home box to close all of its child pages. Notice that the Feedback page remains open because it is a *peer page* of the home page, meaning that it is at the same hierarchical level.

← **Peer pages**

5. Click the More Buttons button on the Standard toolbar to display its palette and then click the Undo button to restore the previous view.

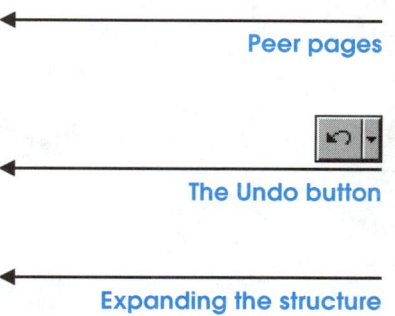

← **The Undo button**

6. Next redisplay the five Service pages by clicking the plus icon on the Services box.

← **Expanding the structure**

Deleting Pages

Now that you know how to move around in navigation view, you can start the reorganization process by deleting a page you don't need. Follow the steps on the next page.

Changing the navigation view

By using the buttons on the Navigation toolbar, you can alter the appearance of your web in navigation view. Use the Zoom box to change the view magnification. (This feature is handy if your web contains several pages and you want to see them all on the screen at once.) Click the Portrait/Landscape button to change the orientation of your web layout. Select a box and then click the External Link button to attach a hyperlink to the box's page, or click the Included In Navigation Bars button to add or remove the page from the web's navigation bars. (We discuss navigation bars on page 21.) Finally, click the View Subtree Only button to display only the selected box and its child pages.

1. Right-click the Service 5 box and choose Delete from the shortcut menu. FrontPage displays this dialog box:

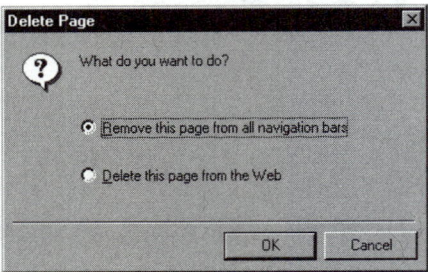

2. Select Delete This Page From The Web and click OK.

Adding Pages

You will often want to add pages to a wizard-generated web. You saw in the previous steps how easy it is to delete pages, and adding pages is just as simple. Follow these steps:

1. Select the Home box and then click the New Page button on the Standard toolbar. FrontPage adds New Page 2 as a child page of the home page.

2. Add a child page to the New Page 2 page by selecting its box and choosing New and then Page from the File menu. Your screen now looks like this:

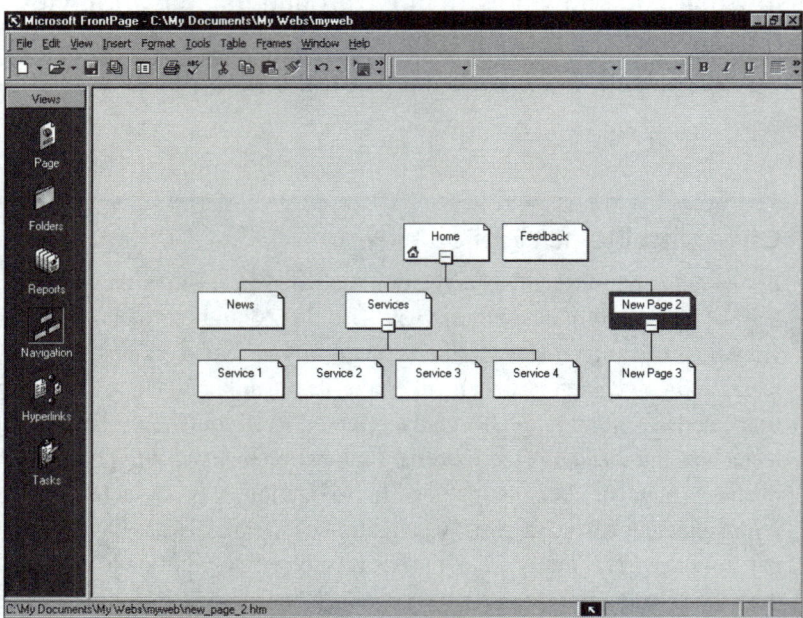

Deleting vs. removing

You can delete a page from the navigation bars (see page 21 for more information) or from the web. Selecting the first option removes the page both from the structure displayed in navigation view and from the navigation bars, but not from the web. However, the page is still available for use. Selecting the second option deletes the page file entirely.

Now let's change the position of these new pages:

1. Point to the News box and drag it to the right of the New Page 2 box. Check that a line connects the page to the home page, indicating that the page will remain a child page of the home page, and then release the mouse button. The News box moves to its new position, as shown here:

Moving pages

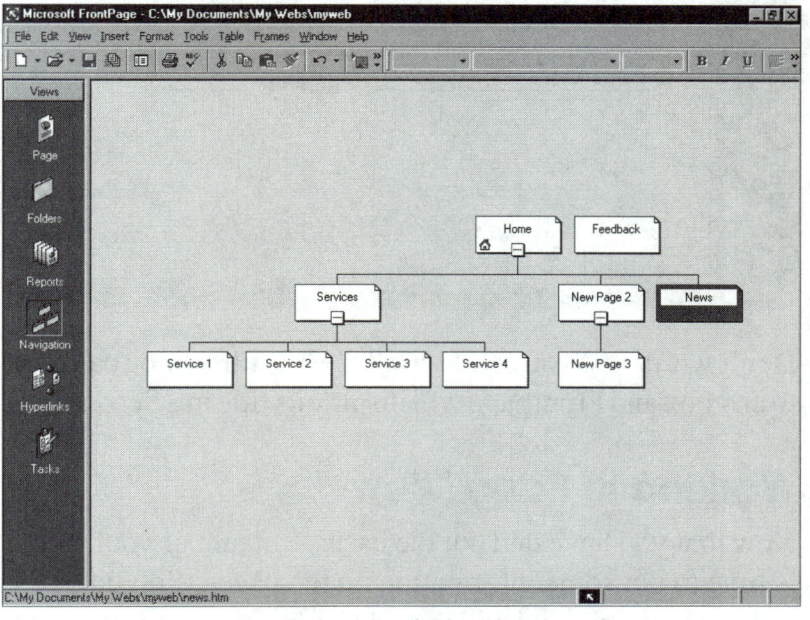

2. Click the New Page 2 box once to select it and then click the title to select its text. Type *What We Provide* and press Enter to retitle the page. (The underlying filename of this page does not change, but the title that appears on the page is updated.)

Renaming pages

3. Next change the title of New Page 3 by right-clicking the box, choosing Rename from the shortcut menu, typing *Resources*, and pressing Enter.

4. Change the Home box's title to *Exotic Excursions* and the Services title to *Our Destinations*.

5. Finally, rename the Service boxes as follows and then turn the page to see the results.

   Service 1   *Serengeti Plain*
   Service 2   *Death Valley*
   Service 3   *Iditarod*
   Service 4   *Kilauea*

Name vs. title

When you rename a page, as you did in the adjacent exercise, you change its title, not its name. The title is what your visitors see when they view the page. Each title should be descriptive enough to tell viewers what that page is about. The name of a web page is its filename, which serves as part of the address of the page. (A computer uses the address to find the page on a server.) On page 28, we show you how to change the page's filename.

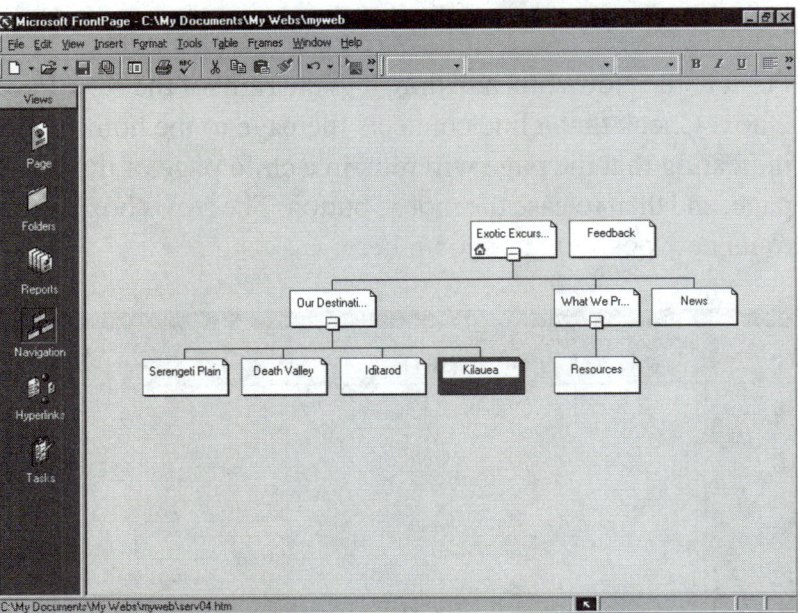

Displaying a title

Don't worry that you can't see all the box titles. You can point to any box and FrontPage will display its title in a ScreenTip.

Working in Page View

Now that you have laid out the basic structure of your web, it is time to put some information on the pages. You do that in page view, which provides a familiar word processor-style environment where you can use editing techniques similar to those you would use in most word processing programs. You can easily add, edit, and format text, as well as insert and manipulate graphics, tables, and other elements. You can also define other features of your web, such as buttons, hyperlinks, and bookmarks. Let's switch to page view now and then start adding information to the Exotic Excursions web:

Switching to page view

1. Double-click the Exotic Excursions box to simultaneously switch to page view and open the home page of the Exotic Excursions web.

2. Click the Folder List button to close the folder list. Your screen now looks like the one on the facing page.

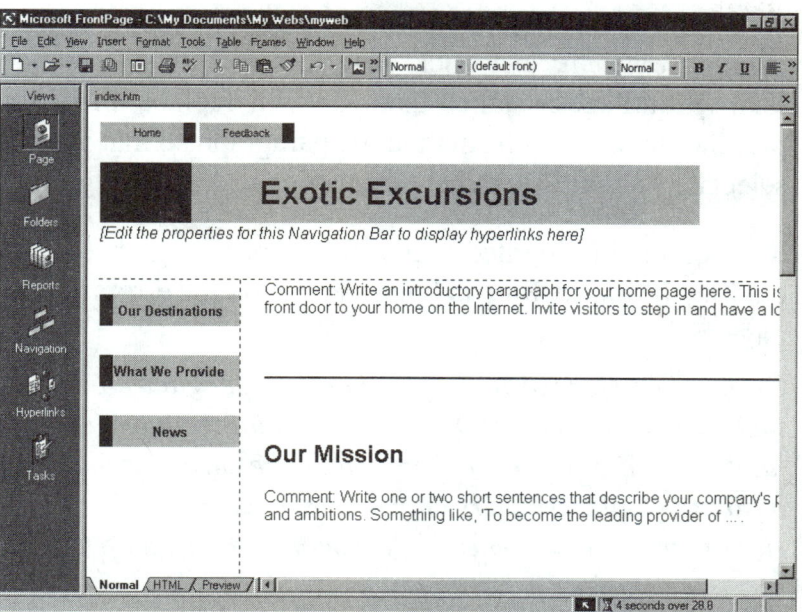

3. Move the pointer over various parts of the page, noticing where it changes shape. As you can see, at the top of the home page is a *navigation bar* containing buttons for the two peer pages: Home and Feedback. These buttons are hyperlinks that are available on all the pages of your web, allowing visitors to jump to either one of those pages from any other page. On the left side of the home page below the title is another navigation bar containing hyperlink buttons for the home page's three child pages: Our Destinations, What We Provide, and News. If you click one of these links, you jump directly to the corresponding page.

Navigation bars

4. Take a few moments to scroll through the home page and notice the headings, which you entered via the Corporate Presence Wizard. The placeholder text after each heading suggests what you might include in each section. Toward the bottom of the page is the contact information that you entered earlier, including the *Send mail to* and *Last modified* items.

Adding and Editing Text

Now that you have a feel for what the page looks like, you are ready to begin adding and editing text. First you'll change the text of the opening paragraph. Turn the page to see the steps.

The home page's filename

The filename of the page currently displayed in the workspace appears in the workspace's title bar. By default, a web's home page is named index.htm. When you display a Web site, the web browser displays index.htm unless it is told to display a different file. So unless you have a very good reason for naming your home page something else, it's best to use the default file name.

Replacing placeholders

1. At the top of the page, point anywhere in the paragraph that begins *Comment:* and click once to select the placeholder text. (FrontPage assumes that you will replace all of this placeholder and has formatted the paragraph so that you can select it by clicking it, rather than having to drag through it.)

2. Replace the highlighted text with the paragraph below, including the misspelling in bold. (You'll fix the errors later on page 58.)

   Exotic Excursions provides exciting, unusual guided bicycle tours around the globe. Our trips aren't for the **novace** *or the faint-hearted. If you have the stamina, the curiosity, and the desire to go places others only dream of, an Exotic Excursions tour will give you enough memories to last a lifetime!*

3. Select the paragraph below the Our Mission heading and type the text below, including the errors in bold:

   Exotic Excursions is **commited** *to providing affordable rides that challenge your sense of adventure without punishing your body or your psyche. We are in constant search of new destinations and, in response to* **you're** *suggestions, will continually endeavor to provide the innovative tours our customers have come to expect.*

   Here are the results:

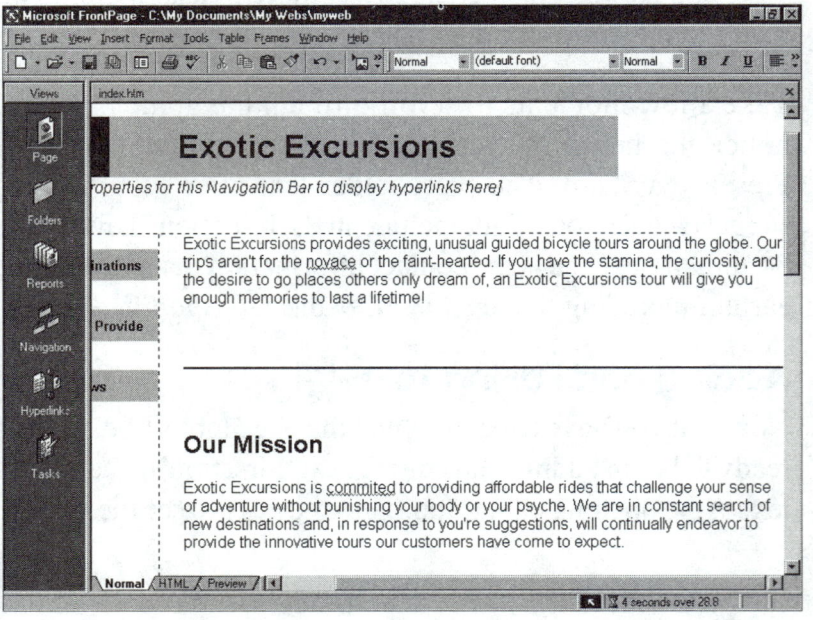

Using text from another source

If you want to reuse an entire file from another source for your web, you can easily insert it. Click an insertion point where you want the file to appear. Then choose File from the Insert menu, navigate to the file you want to insert, and double-click the name. (Be sure that the Files Of Type setting is correct for the file you want to insert.) FrontPage then converts the file to HTML format and inserts it at the location of your insertion point.

4. To save the work you have done so far, click the Save button on the Standard toolbar.

The Save button

5. Now select all the text below the Company Profile heading and type the paragraph below, including the error in bold:

*Wendy Wheeler, president of Exotic Excursions, started the company in 1993 after successfully biking from Seattle to Anchorage. She wanted others to experience the thrills and **beuty** of the trip and decided to start the tour company along with fellow world-class cyclists, Gary Gears and Sandy Spokes. Wheeler, a two-time US cycling champion, still guides some of the tours herself.*

You aren't going to add text below the Contact Information heading, so don't you need to delete the placeholder paragraph? No. Follow along with the next section to see why.

Using the Page View Tabs

So far, you have been working in page view's Normal tab, but you have probably noticed the two other tabs at the bottom of the page view window. Let's take a closer look:

1. Click the Preview tab to simulate viewing your home page in a Web browser. Your screen looks like the one shown here:

The Preview tab

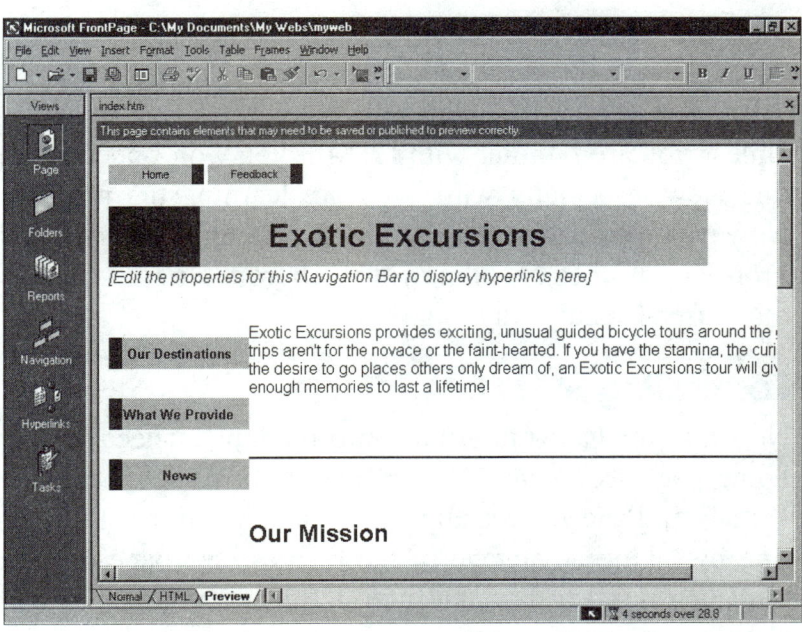

Because you have not added any complex elements to the web yet, the home page looks basically the same when viewed on this tab as it does on the Normal tab.

2. Scroll down the page and look at the Contact Information section. Notice that the placeholder paragraph below the heading is not displayed. Only text you have typed in a wizard dialog box or directly in page view is visible.

The HTML tab

3. Next click the HTML tab to view the home page like this (we've scrolled to the top of the window):

Unless you are familiar with HTML, you won't need to use this view, especially while you are learning the program. However, you can see from a glance at this tab that using FrontPage instead of coding your web from scratch is a much more user-friendly way to go!

Formatting Text

Now that you have most of the information you need on your home page, you can turn your attention to its appearance. With FrontPage you can apply fancy combinations of formatting by taking advantage of the themes (see page 41) and built-in styles (see the adjacent tip). But here you'll stick with simple character formatting. Follow these steps:

Formatting with styles

When you apply a theme to a web, the formatting of your text is controlled by the set of styles that are part of the theme. Each style is a combination of formatting (such as font, size, and color, as well as spacing and alignment) that is applied to a particular element of a page. For example, the H1 style defines how first-level headings should look when displayed by a web browser. You can change the style applied to any paragraph by clicking an insertion point anywhere in it and selecting a different style from the Styles drop-down list on the Formatting toolbar. But be careful. Changing a paragraph's style doesn't just affect the way it looks. It changes its function within the web, too.

1. Click the Normal tab and then select the first paragraph of text that describes Exotic Excursions.

   The Normal tab

2. Click the arrow to the right of the Font box on the Formatting toolbar and then select Times New Roman from the drop-down list.

   Changing the font

3. Next click the arrow to the right of the Font Size box and select 4 (14 pt) from the drop-down list.

   Changing the font size

4. Click the More Buttons button on the Formatting toolbar and then click the arrow to the right of the Font Color button to display a palette of options. In the Theme Colors section, select dark blue. The palette closes, and the Font Color button is now displayed at the end of the Formatting toolbar.

   The Font Color button

5. Press the End key to remove the highlighting. Here are the results:

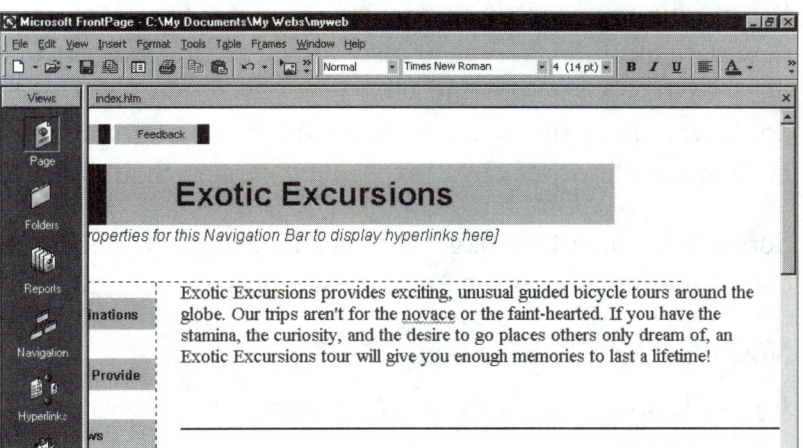

More font options

When experimenting with formatting text, be sure to check out the options available in the Font dialog box. To display this dialog box, select the text you want to format and choose Font from the Format menu. On the Font tab, you can change options that are available on the Formatting toolbar, such as the font, style, size, and color. But you can also select check boxes in the Effects section to format text as blinking, small capped, superscripted, and so on. FrontPage displays a preview of the formatting in the Preview box below. On the Character Spacing tab, you can use the Spacing edit box to change the spacing between characters and the Position edit box to change the position of the text.

Using unusual fonts

When selecting fonts for a web, bear in mind that visitors can see the fonts only if they are installed on their computers. If a font isn't installed, their browser substitutes a similar one. Be careful not to use unusual fonts that have features which can't be easily emulated by the standard fonts found on most people's computers.

Changing Paragraph Alignment

By default, FrontPage left-aligns paragraphs when you set up your pages. However, sometimes you will want to change the alignment of a paragraph or text selection. Follow these steps to center the paragraph at the bottom of the page:

1. Scroll to the bottom of the page and click an insertion point anywhere in the paragraph that begins *Send mail to*. FrontPage displays borders around this and two other sections on the page because they are designated as *shared borders* and appear on every page of the web. (See page 51 for more information.)

Shared borders

The Center button

2. Click More Buttons and then the Center button on the Formatting toolbar. Now this text appears centered on every page where it appears.

Controlling Paragraph Spacing

When you enter text in page view, pressing Enter creates a new paragraph. However, it also adds a blank line between the previous paragraph and your new paragraph. When you don't want the extra space between the two paragraphs, you need to use a line break instead of a new paragraph, like this:

1. Scroll to the top of the page and click an insertion point at the end of the introductory paragraph and press Enter.

2. Now type the following text:

   If you like what you see here, tell others.

Inserting a line break

3. Hold down the Shift key and press Enter. The insertion point moves to the next line without inserting extra space.

4. Now type this:

   If you don't, tell us!

5. Save your work before moving on.

Creating Numbered and Bulleted Lists

You can add two types of lists to your pages: numbered lists or bulleted lists. In this section, you will create a bulleted list on the What We Provide page of your web, but bear in mind that the procedure for creating a numbered list is the same. Follow these steps:

1. Click the Open button on the Standard toolbar to display the Open File dialog box shown here:

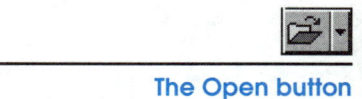
The Open button

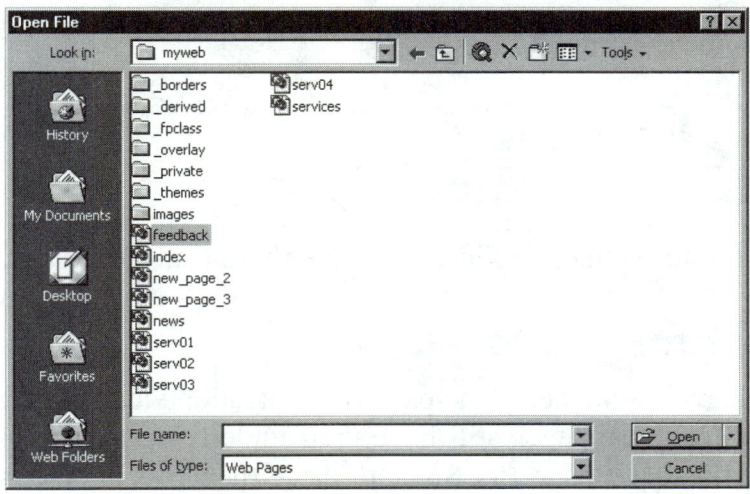

2. Select New_Page_2 in the list of filenames and then click Open to display that page in page view.

3. With the insertion point in the text box adjacent to the *Resources* hyperlink, type the following:

   For every Exotic Excursions tour, we provide the following items:

4. Press Enter and type the items, pressing Enter after each one:

   Meals
   First-Aid and Emergency Repair Equipment
   Camping Gear

5. Select all three items and click More Buttons and then the Bullets button on the Formatting toolbar. FrontPage places a bullet in front of each name, changes the line spacing, and adjusts the text size to match the size of the bullet.

The Bullets button

6. Press End to see the results shown on the next page.

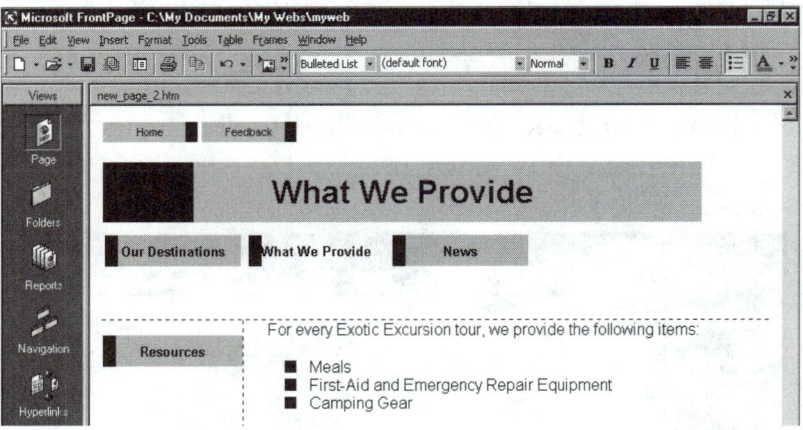

7. Save your changes by clicking the Save button on the toolbar.

Renaming Files

Earlier you renamed some pages in navigation view, but the files for those pages still have their underlying filenames (see the tip on page 19). Some of those filenames are pretty cryptic, so now would be a good time to change them. Follow these steps:

1. Click the Folder List button on the Standard toolbar to open the folder list to the left of the workspace.

2. Right-click new_page_2.htm and choose Rename from the shortcut menu.

> **Changing the bullet character**
>
> The bullet character is controlled by the theme applied to your web. If no theme is applied, you can easily change the bullet character. Select the bulleted items, right-click the selection, and choose List Properties from the shortcut menu to display the List Properties dialog box. Click an option and then click OK. If the choices available on the Plain Bullets tab of the List Properties dialog box don't meet your needs, you can simply click the Image Bullets tab to locate additional bullet images.

3. Type *What_We_Provide.htm* as the new name and press Enter. Because this page is linked to other pages in the web, FrontPage displays this dialog box to prevent you from accidentally breaking the links:

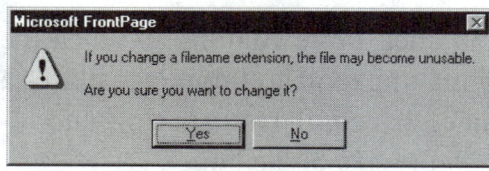

4. Click Yes to have FrontPage update all links that point to New_Page_2 so that they now point to What_We_Provide.

Chapter 1 Creating a Simple Web Site

5. Repeat steps 2, 3, and 4 to rename the new_page_3.htm file as *Resources.htm*.

6. Click the Folder List button to close the list.

   Notice that you used versions of the pages' titles as their filenames to make them easy to recognize. Notice also that you used initial capital letters for your filenames to distinguish them from the default lowercase names assigned by FrontPage.

Getting Help

This tour of FrontPage has covered a lot of ground in just a few pages, and you might be wondering how you will manage to retain it all. Don't worry. If you forget how to carry out a particular task, help is never far away. You've already seen how the ScreenTips feature can jog your memory about the functions of the toolbar buttons. And you may have noticed that the dialog boxes contain a Help button (the ? in the top right corner), which you can click to get information about their options. Here, you'll look at ways to get information using the Help feature. Follow these steps:

1. Click More Buttons and then the Microsoft FrontPage Help button on the Standard toolbar to display the Help window shown here:

The Microsoft FrontPage Help button

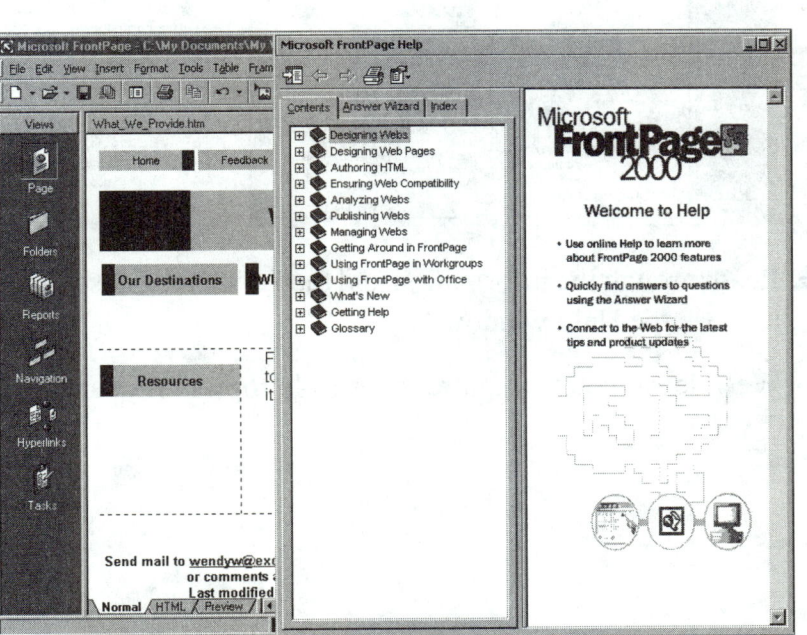

The Contents tab of the Help window organizes topics into categories that are represented by book icons. You can display a category's topics by clicking its plus sign. You can click a topic (designated by a question mark icon) to display its information in the right pane of the Help window.

Using the index

2. Click the Index tab and type *bullet* in the Type Keywords box. The list below scrolls to display topics beginning with the letters you type.

3. Click the Search button. Now the Choose A Topic list displays topics that deal with the word you have typed.

4. Click *Create a bulleted list* to display the information shown here in the right pane:

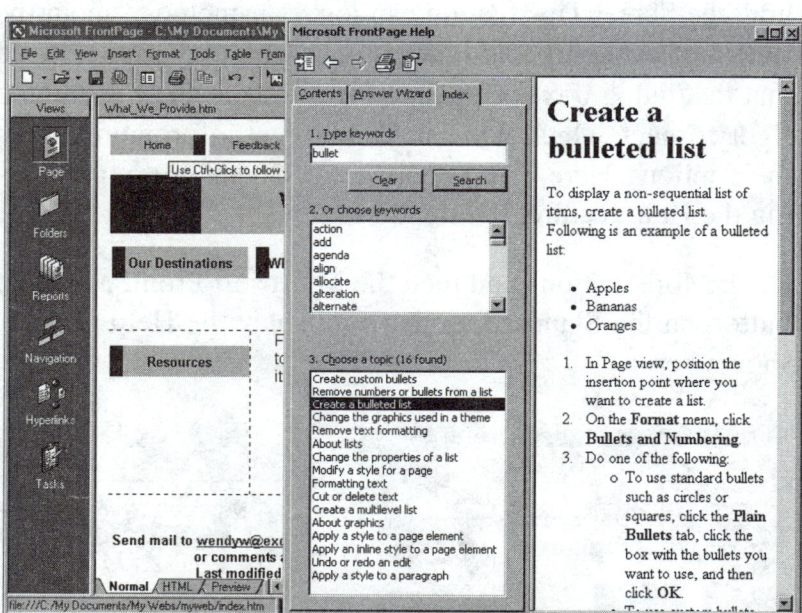

Other ways to get help

The Answer Wizard provides a way to ask questions in plain language. Click the Answer Wizard tab, type a question in the edit box, and click Search. When Help displays a list of the topics that most closely address your question, you can click one of the topics to display its contents in the right pane of the Help window. If you have a modem and are connected to the Internet, you can access the Microsoft Web site to get information or technical support. Choose Office On The Web from the Help menu to start your Web browser, connect to the Internet, and display the site. From there, you can navigate to the information you need.

5. Read through the information and then click the Close button to close the Help window.

We'll leave you to explore other Help topics on your own.

Quitting FrontPage

You have seen how to use FrontPage to create a simple text-based web. Easy, wasn't it? All that's left is to show you how to end a FrontPage session. Follow these steps:

1. Choose Exit from the File menu.

2. If asked whether you want to save the changes you have made to the open web page, click Yes.

Here are some other ways to quit FrontPage:

- Click the Close button at the right end of FrontPage's title bar.

- Press Alt, then F (the underlined letter in *File* on the menu bar), and then X (the underlined letter in *Exit* on the File menu).

- Double-click the Control menu icon (the sheet of paper with the arrow symbol) at the left end of FrontPage's title bar.

2

Enhancing Your Web

In this chapter, we look at some of the more complex elements you can add to a web. First you add graphics and a theme to give your pages some pizazz. Next you create various types of hyperlinks and bookmarks. Finally, you learn how to work with navigation bars.

Though the sample web you create here is fairly simple, you'll see how to use graphics, themes, hyperlinks, bookmarks, and navigation bars to create more complex webs that visitors can navigate with ease.

Web pages created and concepts covered:

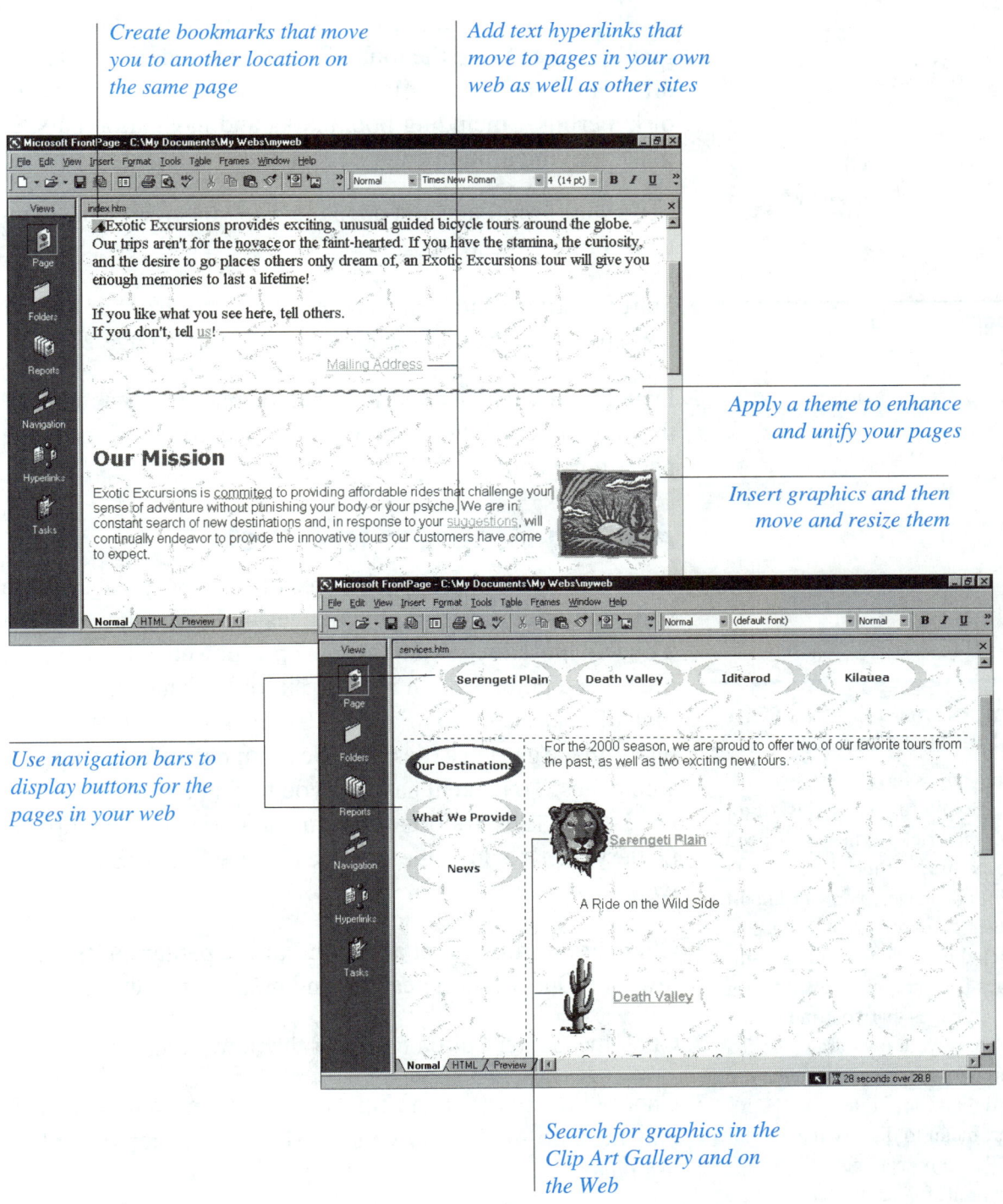

You have now successfully built your first FrontPage web and should be familiar with the basic techniques for modifying it. In this chapter, you will add some graphics to enhance the look of your web, and you'll apply a different theme. You will also see how to add various types of hyperlinks, including bookmarks and navigation bars, to make moving around your web a breeze.

Let's start FrontPage and open the web you created in Chapter 1. Follow these steps:

Opening a web

1. Start FrontPage and then click the Open button on the toolbar to display the Open File dialog box shown on page 27.

2. Double-click the Myweb folder to display its contents, and then double-click the index.htm filename to display the home page in page view.

Adding Graphics to a Web

One of the most attractive features of many web pages is the inclusion of colorful graphic images and even photographs. You will most likely want to dress up your web with images to illustrate a point, sell an idea, or simply enhance the overall look of your web. FrontPage 2000 comes with a collection of ready-made graphics files suitable for many different types of web pages. To make it easy for you to find exactly what you need, these files are organized in categories in the Clip Art Gallery. Let's add some graphics to the Exotic Excursions web now:

1. Click an insertion point at the end of the paragraph that follows the Our Mission heading and press Enter twice.

2. Click the Center button to center the new paragraph.

3. Choose Picture and then Clip Art from the Insert menu to display the Clip Art Gallery window shown at the top of the facing page.

Importing graphics from other sources

Sometimes the clip art available in the Clip Art Gallery just won't do the trick. When you need something other than simple clip art images, you can import other types of graphic images, including scanned images, images from graphic collections on CD, images that you find on the Web, or your own drawings. To import a graphic, choose Picture and then From File from the Insert menu to display the Picture dialog box. Navigate to the appropriate folder and double-click the filename to import the graphic at the location of the insertion point.

Chapter 2 Enhancing Your Web

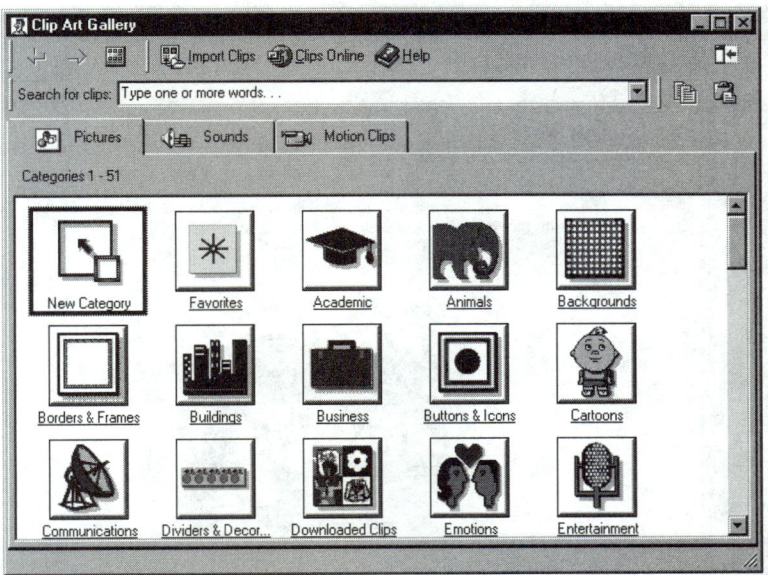

As you can see, the available clip art is divided into categories on the Pictures tab of the Clip Art Gallery window. (You can also click the Sounds tab to display available sound options or the Motion Clips tab to insert a graphic that moves or changes in some way. See page 114.) To see more categories at once, you can click the window's Maximize button, or you can make the window larger or smaller by dragging its frame.

4. Scroll through the categories and then click the Weather category to display its contents.

5. Scroll the window to see the graphics available in this category and then click the Back button or All Categories button to return to the category list.

The Back button and All Categories button

6. Check out any other categories that interest you, and then click the Nature category.

7. Click the graphic of the sun and mountain scene. A palette of buttons appears, allowing you to insert the graphic, preview it, add it to the Favorites category, and find other similar graphics.

8. Click the Insert Clip button on the palette. You return to the home page, where FrontPage has inserted the graphic as shown on the next page.

The Insert Clip button

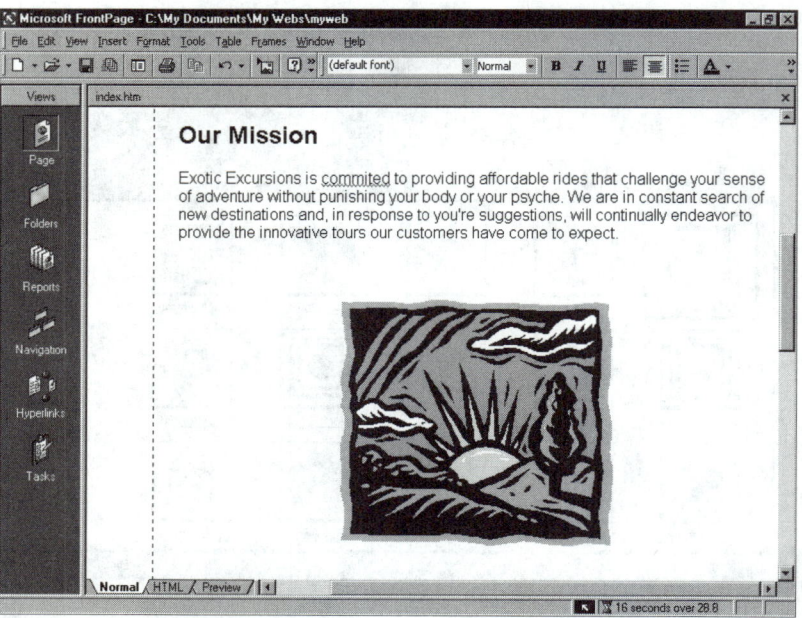

The graphic is too big, and it's not exactly where you want it, so next we'll look at how to size and position graphics.

Sizing and Positioning Graphics

Once you add a graphic or similar object to a page, you can easily make it bigger or smaller and place it where you want it. Follow these steps to change the size and location of the sun graphic:

Selection handles

1. Select the graphic by clicking it. FrontPage surrounds the graphic with small black squares called *handles*.

2. To decrease the graphic's height and width, point to the bottom right handle. When the pointer changes to a double-headed arrow, drag it upward and to the left until the graphic is about 1½ inches high.

If you drag the corner handles, you change the size of the graphic without changing the ratio of its width to its height. If you drag the handles in the middle of the sides of the frame, you do change this ratio. See the tip on the facing page for information about how to control the width-to-height ratio more precisely.

Now let's fine-tune the position of the graphic:

> **Resampling graphics**
>
> If you make a graphic smaller, the graphic on the page changes but the graphic in the underlying file remains the same size. If you want the file size to match the displayed size so that displaying the graphic takes less time, you need to resample the graphic. Size the graphic as you want it and then click the Resample button on the Picture toolbar.

1. With the graphic selected, right-click it, choose Picture Properties from the shortcut menu, and click the Appearance tab to display these options:

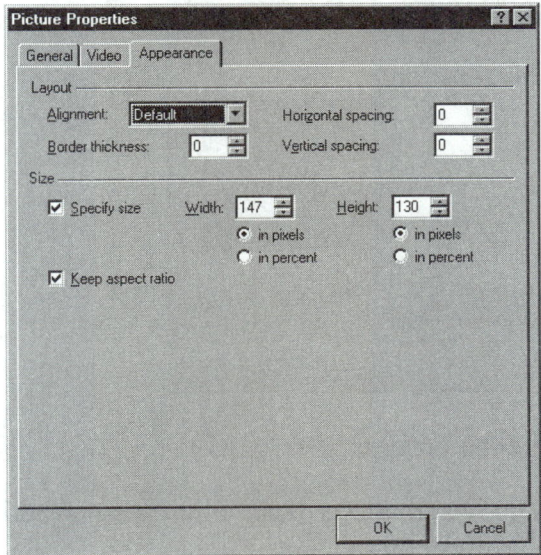

Here, you can determine how you want a graphic aligned on the page, as well as the horizontal or vertical distance between the edge of the graphic and any text. In the Size section, you can enter exact size specifications (see the adjacent the tip).

2. Click the arrow to the right of the Alignment box in the Layout section, select Right from the drop-down list, and click OK.

3. With the graphic still selected, drag upward until the shadow insertion point appears to the right of the Our Mission heading. Then release the mouse button to see these results:

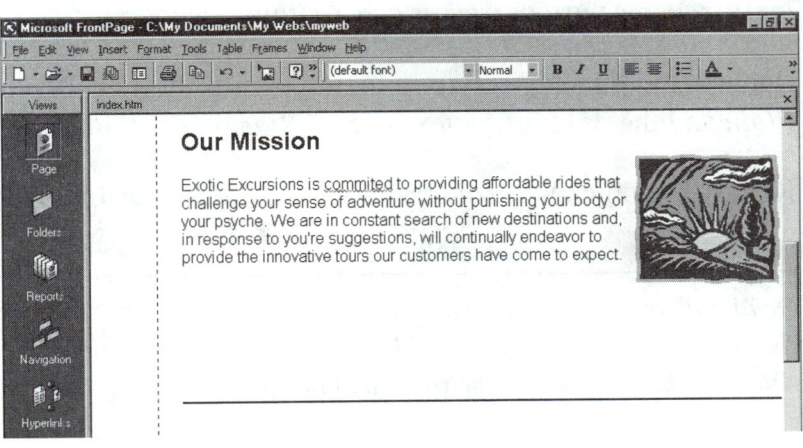

More precise sizing

To make a graphic you have added to a web page a specific size, right-click the graphic and choose Picture Properties from the shortcut menu. On the Appearance tab, select the Specify Size option in the Size section. To maintain the height-to-width ratio, select the Keep Aspect Ratio option; to allow one to change without the other, deselect it. Then select either the In Pixels or In Percent options below the Width and Height boxes to tell FrontPage what type of measurement to use for the new sizes. Finally, change the settings in the Width and Height boxes to the size you want.

Saving embedded graphics

4. Click the Save button on the toolbar. FrontPage displays this dialog box because the graphic has not yet been saved as part of your web:

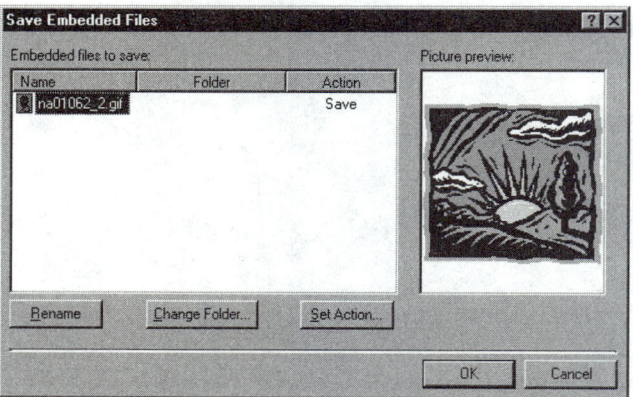

5. Click OK to complete the process.

Now let's set up the Our Destinations page so that you can add some graphics there. Follow these steps:

Opening a page

1. Click the Folder List button on the toolbar to open the folder list. (Notice that the list now includes the graphic you inserted on the home page.)

2. Double-click the services.htm filename to display the Our Destinations page. Then click the Folder List button again to close the list.

3. Click the paragraph that begins *Comment* to select it, and then type the following text:

   For the 2000 season, we are proud to offer two of our favorite tours from the past, as well as two exciting new tours.

Graphic formats

The Graphics Interchange Format (GIF) and Joint Photographic Experts Group (JPEG or JPG) formats are commonly used in web pages because most Web browsers can display them. They also have the advantage of being compressed to save transmission time and storage space.

4. Replace the *Name of service 1* text hyperlink with *Serengeti Plain* and the description text with *A Ride on the Wild Side*.

5. Replace the other *Name of service* placeholders with this text:

Service	Description
Death Valley	Can You Take the Heat?
Iditarod	It's a Dog's Ride!
Kilauea	To the Brink and Back

6. Save your work. (From now on, we won't always remind you to save, but be sure to do so frequently.)

With that bit of set up work out of the way, you can add another graphic.

Searching for Graphics

If you know what type of graphic you are looking for but don't want to spend time searching through each category, you can use the Search For Clips edit box in the Clip Art Gallery window. Follow these steps:

1. Click an insertion point to the right of Serengeti Plain and choose Picture and then Clip Art from the Insert menu.

2. Click the Search For Clips edit box, type *lion*, and press Enter. FrontPage displays the graphics that meet your criteria.

   Entering keywords

3. Click the graphic of a lion's head and then click the Insert Clip button.

4. Resize the graphic, making it about 1 inch in height. Then display the Picture Properties dialog box and on the Appearance tab, change the graphic's alignment to Absmiddle (*absolute middle*). Click OK to see these results:

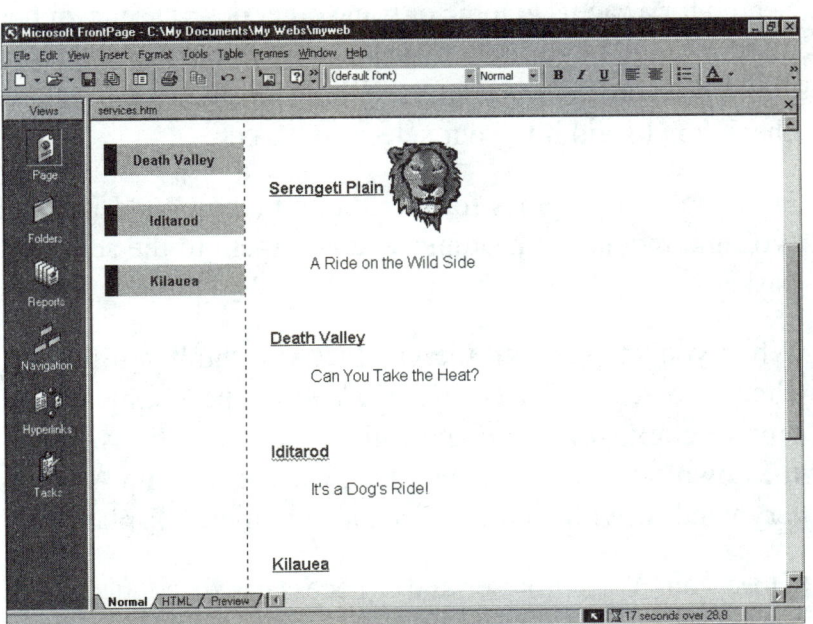

Clip art keywords

All the graphics in the Clip Art Gallery window have been assigned keywords that describe their contents. If you point to a graphic and pause, these keywords appear in a pop-up box. To find a particular graphic, you can enter as many keywords as you want in the Search For Clips edit box, separating them with commas.

5. On second thought, the graphic would look better to the left of its heading. Select the graphic and drag it into place.

Searching for Graphics on the Web

If the results of a search don't identify a graphic you can use, you can always enter a different word in the Search For Clips edit box. However, the graphics included in the Clip Art Gallery are somewhat limited, so you may want to search elsewhere for more graphics. One of the best ways to search is by using Microsoft's Clip Gallery Live Web page. Fortunately, you can easily access this page from the Clip Art Gallery window. Follow these steps to search for a graphic online:

The Clip Gallery Live Web page

1. Click an insertion point to the left of Death Valley and then choose Picture and Clip Art from the Insert menu.

The Clips Online button

2. Click the Clips Online button on the Clip Art Gallery toolbar. Windows starts Internet Explorer or your Web browser and may prompt you to connect to your ISP. Once connected, the browser displays the Clip Gallery Live Web page.

3. Read the license agreement and click Accept. Then click Yes if Internet Explorer warns that information you send over the Internet may be seen by others.

Selecting graphics to download

4. Search for a cactus graphic or some other desert scene, either by browsing categories or by entering keywords and clicking Go. When you find what you're looking for, click the graphic's check box to add it to your selection basket.

5. Now look for graphics for the Iditarod (snow) and Kilauea (volcano/mountain) headings and add them to the selection basket.

Downloading graphics

6. When you've found all the graphics you think you'll need, click the *Selection Basket* hyperlink above the graphics. Then simply click *Download* and follow the instructions. When the download process is complete, you see the Clip Art Gallery window with all the downloaded graphics displayed.

7. Close your Web browser and if necessary, disconnect from the Internet.

Now let's add the downloaded graphics to your web page:

1. Insert the cactus or desert graphic to the left of the Desert Valley heading. Then size and position the graphic so that it matches the lion graphic above.

2. Next insert the graphics you downloaded for the Iditarod and Kilauea tours next to their headings. (You'll find them in the Downloaded Clips category.) Size and position these graphics to match the others. Here are the results:

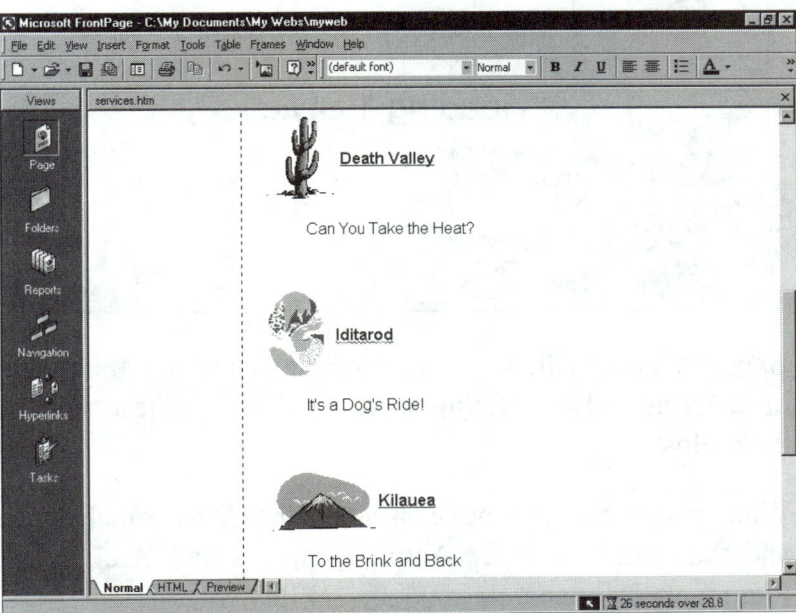

3. Click the Save button to display the Save Embedded Files dialog box and then click OK. The images you have added are now included in your web.

Applying a Different Theme

So far, the Exotic Excursions web is fairly plain other than the few graphics you have added. For some types of web pages, a white background with a few frills will work just fine, but for a company trying to promote exciting, off-the-beaten-track bicycle tours, you want something more lively. With FrontPage, you can apply one of several predefined themes that add elements such as a graphic background, buttons, and a color scheme to your web. Let's find a theme for the Exotic Excursions web now. Follow the steps on the next page.

Background formatting

To change the background without using a theme, right-click a blank area of the page and choose Page Properties from the shortcut menu. On the Background tab, click Background Picture and select an image file, or select a color from the Background drop-down list. Click More Colors to display additional options. You can also click Get Background Information From Another Page at the bottom of the dialog box to apply the background and colors of one page to another.

Switching the active page

1. Choose index.htm, the filename of the home page, from the Window menu to redisplay that page.

2. Choose Theme from the Format menu to display the dialog box shown here:

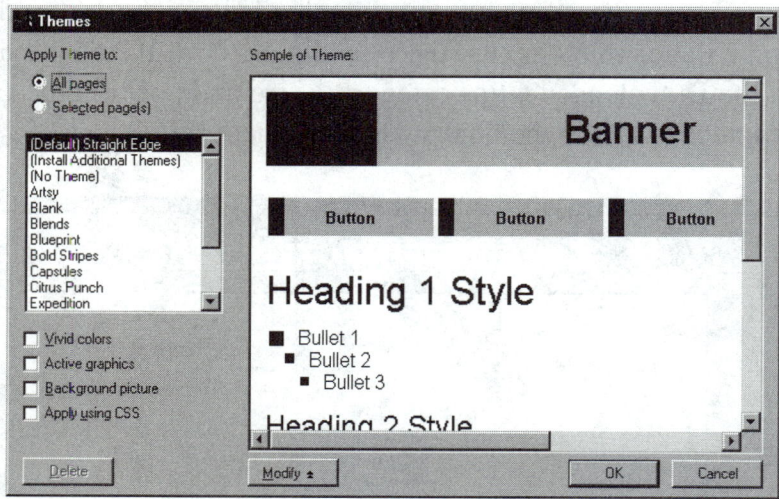

3. Experiment with the various themes and check out the effects of selecting and deselecting the check boxes on the left side of the dialog box.

4. When you're ready to move on, select the Citrus Punch theme and then click both the Active Graphics and Background Picture check boxes.

Modifying themes

You can change a theme by selecting it in the Themes dialog box and clicking the Modify button. Next click either the Colors, Graphics, or the Text button and make changes to that element. Once you have made all the modifications you want, click the Save As button to display the Save Theme dialog box. (You can't change the settings of a predefined theme.) Enter a name for the new theme and click OK.

No theme on a page

In some instances, you may not want one of your web's pages to use the theme you have applied. To remove the theme, display the page, right-click a blank area, and choose Theme from the shortcut menu to display a dialog box similar to the one shown above. With the Selected Page(s) option selected, click No Theme in the themes list and then click OK.

Cascading style sheets

Because HTML was not designed to be a page-layout program, in the past it was difficult to control the position and the look of items on the screen. Cascading style sheets were invented to solve this problem. You don't need to know about cascading style sheets to use FrontPage themes. But if you're interested, you might want to check out this topic in the Help feature.

5. To apply the theme to all pages of the web, check that All Pages is selected and then click OK. Here are the results:

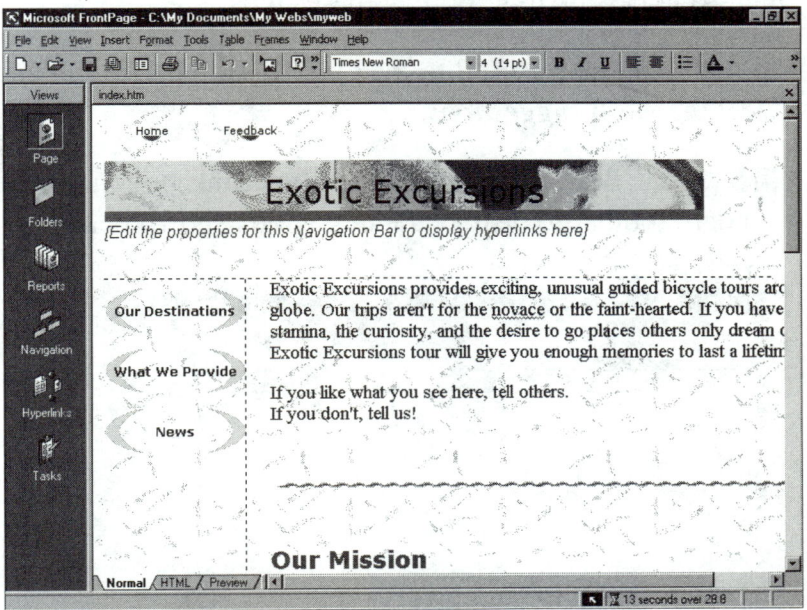

Notice that the introductory paragraph has retained the formatting you applied in Chapter 1.

Adding Hyperlinks

One of the greatest features of the Web is the capability of quickly traveling to any other Web site in the world with just a click of the mouse. This ease of movement is made possible by hyperlinks, which are pointers that store the address (or location) of an object called the *target*. The target is usually another Web page that is either part of the current Web site or located on a totally different site, but it can also be an image, a sound clip, or even a movie snippet.

Targets

You have seen that when you use a FrontPage wizard to create a web, the wizard adds hyperlinks between the web's pages. However, you will probably want to add or change links as your web evolves. In this section, we show you several types of *text hyperlinks* and how to add and edit them. Text hyperlinks are represented by a word or phrase on a page and are the simplest and most common type of hyperlink.

Text hyperlinks

Linking to a New Page

First let's add a new page to the Exotic Excursions web and create a hyperlink to it. Follow these steps:

1. On the home page, scroll to the Our Mission paragraph and select the word *suggestions*.

The Hyperlink button

2. Click More Buttons and then the Hyperlink button on the Standard toolbar to display the dialog box shown below:

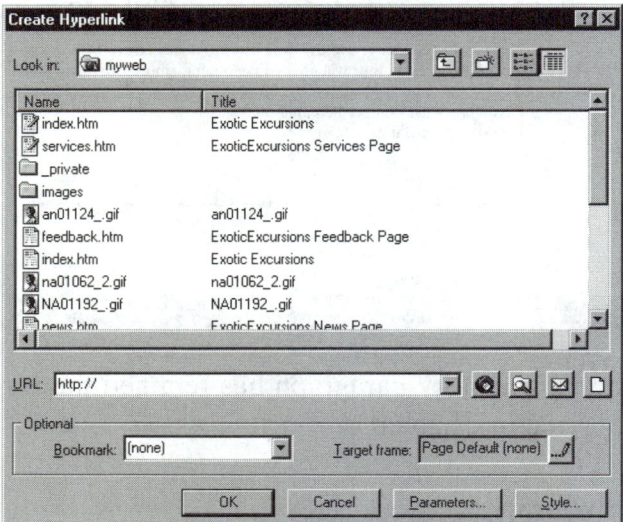

Here you can view a list of all of the folders and pages that make up your web.

The Create A Page And Link To The New Page button

3. You want to create a link to a page that doesn't yet exist, so click the Create A Page And Link To The New Page button to the right of the URL box. FrontPage displays the dialog box shown on the facing page.

URLs

Every Web site has a *uniform resource locator (URL)* that identifies the protocol your browser must use and the computer on which the site's files are stored. A typical URL starts with *http* (for HyperText Transfer Protocol) followed by *www* (for World Wide Web), followed by the site's domain name (which is associated with a specific Web server). The domain name might be followed by the directory and filename of a specific page at the site. (You have to type the *http* part of a URL only if the site's address doesn't begin with *www*.)

Chapter 2 Enhancing Your Web

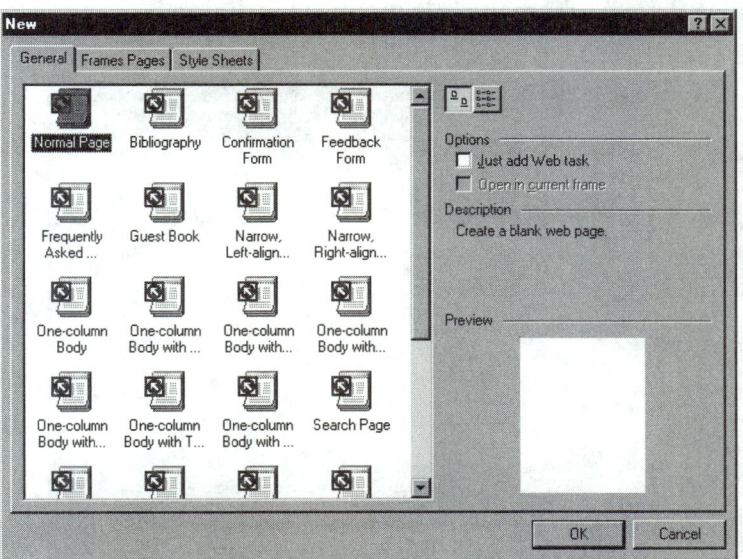

4. Click the Feedback Form icon on the General tab and click OK. FrontPage displays a new page like this one:

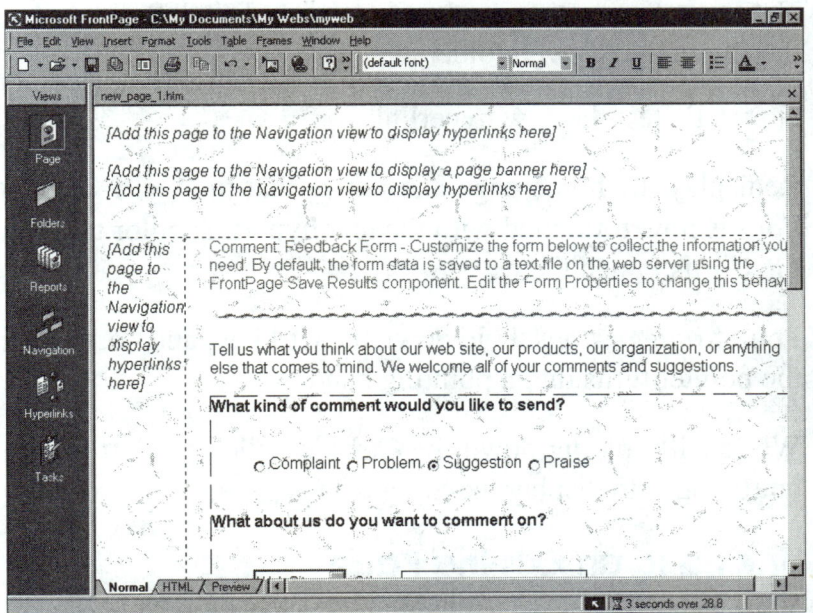

5. Next select the paragraph that begins *Tell us* and type:

   We welcome your suggestions for possible new tours to add to our current list of destinations.

Recognizing text hyperlinks

Experienced Web users recognize text that is blue and underlined as a hyperlink. They also recognize text that is purple and underlined as a hyperlink that has already been visited. If you are not using a theme, FrontPage assigns these default colors. Although you can change the colors using the Background tab of the Page Properties dialog box (see the tip on page 41), doing so could confuse your visitors, so be cautious about this kind of change. If you are using a theme, FrontPage may assign different text hyperlink colors, which you can change by modifying the theme (see page 42). Recent versions of Web browsers display the target address of a hyperlink when you move your pointer over it, providing visitors with yet another way to recognize a hyperlink.

Saving a new page

6. Choose Save As from the File menu. This dialog box appears:

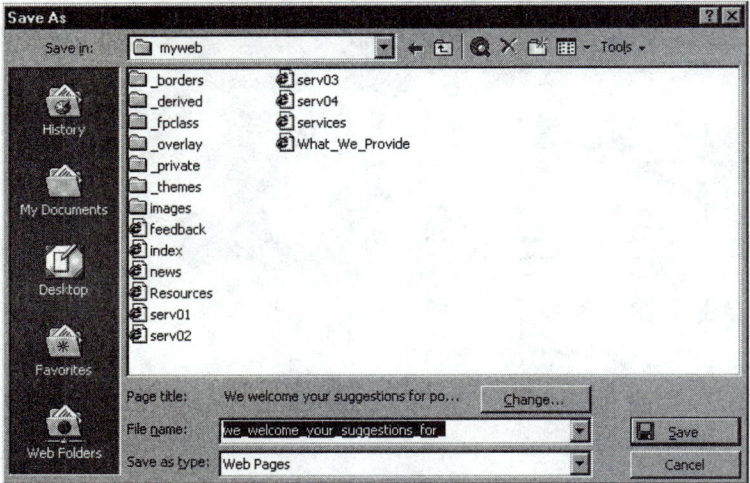

7. Click the Change button to the right of the Page Title section, type *Suggestions*, and click OK.

8. Next type *Suggestions* as the filename and click Save to save the file in the Myweb folder.

Now let's test the new hyperlink:

Testing internal hyperlinks

1. Redisplay the home page and notice that the word *suggestions* is now formatted with the text hyperlink color used by the Citrus Punch theme.

2. Point to *suggestions*, hold down the Ctrl key, and notice that the pointer turns into a pointing hand.

3. While still holding down the Ctrl key, click the left mouse button once to display the Suggestions page.

Linking to an Existing Page

Your web now has a page that invites visitors to suggest possible new bike tours, but it would be nice to add a link to the list of tours that are currently available. Follow these steps to add the link now:

1. With the Suggestions page displayed, select *destinations* in the paragraph you just typed and click the Hyperlink button on the toolbar.

2. In the Create Hyperlink dialog box, click services.htm in the list of files to add its filename to the URL box. Then click OK.

3. If you want, test the new link to verify that it moves you to the Our Destinations page.

Adding E-Mail Hyperlinks

One type of text hyperlink commonly used in web pages is the e-mail address hyperlink. Because you used a FrontPage wizard in Chapter 1, the Exotic Excursions web already has links that allow visitors to send e-mail directly to Wendy Wheeler. You can easily add other e-mail hyperlinks, also referred to as *mailto hyperlinks*, to your pages so that visitors can conveniently communicate with you. Follow these steps:

Mailto hyperlinks

1. Display the home page and select the word *us* in *If you don't, tell us*.

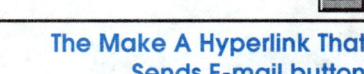

The Make A Hyperlink That Sends E-mail button

2. Choose Hyperlink from the Insert menu and click the Make A Hyperlink That Sends E-mail button to the right of the URL box to display this dialog box:

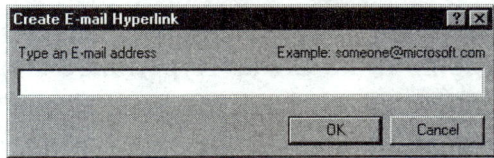

3. Type *info@exoticexcursions.tld* in the Type An E-mail Address box and click OK. FrontPage adds the address to the URL box in the Create Hyperlink dialog box and adds *mailto:* in front of it. Click OK again to create the hyperlink.

Testing mailto hyperlinks

4. If e-mail is set up on your computer, test the new mailto hyperlink by clicking the Preview tab and then clicking the link. Your e-mail program starts and opens a message window with the hyperlink's e-mail address already inserted in the To edit box, ready for you to send a message.

5. Click the Close button to close the window without sending a message and if necessary, close your e-mail program. Then click the Normal tab.

6. Save your changes.

Adding Links to Other Web Sites

So far, we have shown you several ways to use hyperlinks to make it easier to move around your web. However, to make your web really useful, you will most likely want to link it to other Web sites. Thankfully, this task is as easy as creating any other hyperlink. For this example, you will create a link on the Resources page to the site maintained by the International Cycling Union. Let's get started:

1. Display the folder list, double-click the Resources file, and then close the folder list again.

2. At the insertion point, type the following, including the misspelling in bold:

   *To get ready for an Exotic Excursions **toor**, you might want to check out one of these resources for training tips and information about the latest in cycling gear:*

3. Press Enter and type *International Cycling Union*.

4. Select the association name and click the Hyperlink button on the toolbar.

5. After *http://* in the URL box of the Create Hyperlink dialog box, type *www.uci.ch/english/* and click OK. (This site doesn't actually have training or equipment information, but it's a great source of information about cycle racing world wide.)

That was easy enough because you were given the Web site's URL. What do you do if you don't know the URL? You can find the Web resources you need for your web without leaving FrontPage. For demonstration purposes, let's add another link to the list of resources. Although it has nothing to do with cycling, we'll use our own Web site as an example. Try this:

1. Click an insertion point at the end of the *International Cycling Union* line and press Enter.

2. Type *Online Press Inc.*, select the text, and click the Hyperlink button on the toolbar.

Adding graphic hyperlinks

When a word or phrase won't do the trick, you can use a graphic image to create a fancier hyperlink. For example, you can use scanned pictures or digital photographs. To create the hyperlink, select the graphic and click the Hyperlink button on the Standard toolbar. In the list of files, select the page you want the hyperlink to jump to or enter an address in the URL box. Then click OK.

Chapter 2 Enhancing Your Web

3. Click the Use Your Web Browser To Select A Page Or File button to the right of the URL box.

The Use Your Web Browser To Select A Page Or File button

4. Connect to the Internet if you are prompted. You then see your Web browser's starting page.

5. Type *www.yahoo.com* in the Address bar and press Enter to move to one of the best-known Web search services.

6. In the Search text box, type *quick course* and click Search. The results of your search look something like those shown here:

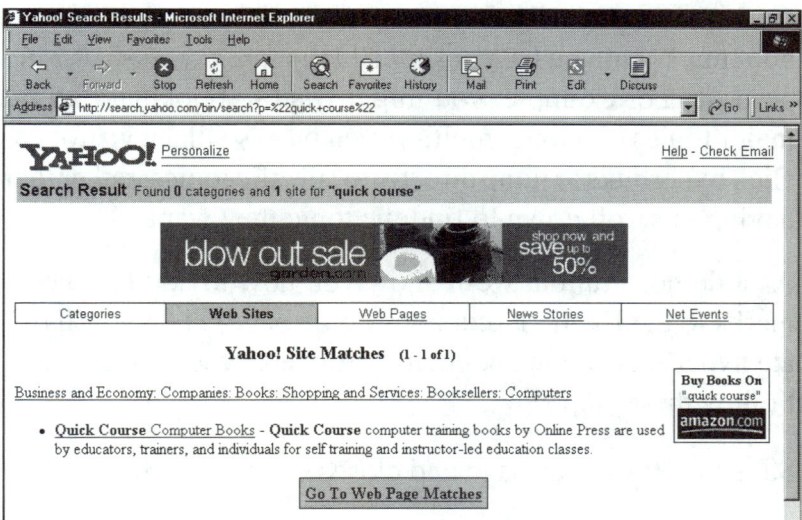

7. Click the hyperlink that takes you to the Quick Course site maintained by Online Press. (The URL should be *http://www.quickcourse.com* or *http://www.qkcourse.com.*)

8. Click the FrontPage button on the Windows taskbar. The Create Hyperlink dialog box is displayed, with the address for the Quick Course home page entered in the URL box.

9. Click OK. Then close your Web browser and if necessary, disconnect from the Internet.

10. Test the hyperlink by holding down the Ctrl key and clicking. If prompted, connect to the Internet. After checking out the target page in the FrontPage workspace, click the workspace Close button (above the vertical scroll bar) and if necessary, disconnect again.

Testing external hyperlinks

Adding Links to Bookmarks

You may think of a bookmark as some long, flat object that is used to mark your place in a printed book. More recently, this term has been used by some Web browsers to refer to a location on the Web that you have marked for a return visit. (Internet Explorer uses the term *favorite* instead of *bookmark*.) In FrontPage, a bookmark, which is also called an *anchor*, has the more traditional meaning.

Favorites

Clicking a regular hyperlink takes you to the top of a particular page. But suppose you want to jump to a specific location on the same page. Then you need to create a hyperlink to a bookmark that you have inserted in the text expressly for this purpose. For example, you might want to bookmark all the major topics of a long, multi-screen page so that a visitor can click hyperlinks to jump directly to specific topics, rather than having to scroll down to find the topic they want.

As a demonstration, we'll show you how to add two bookmarks to the Exotic Excursions home page. Then you'll create hyperlinks to the bookmarks from elsewhere on the page. Follow these steps:

1. Save the Resources page and close it.

Bookmarking locations

2. Display the home page and click an insertion point to the left of the *E* in *Exotic Excursions* in the opening paragraph.

3. Choose Bookmark from the expanded Insert menu to display the dialog box shown here:

> **Removing bookmarks**
>
> You can easily remove a bookmark. Select the bookmarked text, right-click it, and choose Bookmark Properties from the shortcut menu to display the Bookmark dialog box. Then with the bookmark name selected, click the Clear button. FrontPage clears the bookmark, but leaves the text that represented it on the page. If you inserted a bookmark without selecting text, you will then have to delete the flag icon.

4. Type *The Top* in the Bookmark Name edit box and click OK. (If you select text before choosing the Bookmark command, that text appears in the Bookmark Name edit box.) FrontPage inserts a bookmark icon (a blue flag) where the insertion point is located.

5. Scroll down the page to the phone and address section. Click an insertion point at the end of the Webmaster's e-mail address and press Enter twice to start a new line with some extra space above it.

6. Type *Return to Top*, select the text, and then click the Center button.

7. With the text still selected, click the Hyperlink button.

8. Click the arrow to the right of the Bookmark box in the Optional section, select The Top from the drop-down list, and click OK.

9. Now select the entire address under *Postal address* and create a bookmark called *Mailing Address*. FrontPage underlines the selection with dashes. ⬅ **Bookmarking existing text**

10. Scroll to the top of the page and click an insertion point between the introductory text and the wavy, horizontal bar.

11. Type *Mailing Address* and center the text. Then create a hyperlink that jumps to the Mailing Address bookmark.

12. Hold down the Ctrl key and click each bookmark in turn to check whether it jumps to the correct place on the page. ⬅ **Testing bookmarks**

Working with Navigation Bars

Before we end this chapter, we want to discuss navigation bars, which offer yet another way for visitors to move around your site. Because you used a wizard to create the Exotic Excursions web, FrontPage has already included navigation bars in the shared border regions of each page. (As we mentioned earlier, a shared border is an area that can appear on each page of a web.) However, the buttons in the navigation bars need some reorganization. First make some adjustments in navigation view by following these steps:

1. Switch to navigation view by clicking the Navigation icon on the Views bar. The way the web is laid out in this view determines which navigation buttons are added to the web's various shared borders. The top shared border displays buttons for the top level of the web's structure (the Exotic Excursions and Feedback pages). The left shared border displays buttons for the three child pages of the home page (the Our Destinations, What We Provide, and News pages). Since you last worked in navigation view, you have added a new page to the web, and you now need to add it to the structure.

Adding pages to the navigation structure

2. Display the folder list, select Suggestions.htm and drag it between the Exotic Excursions and Feedback boxes. FrontPage attaches the new page with a line above the Exotic Excursions box to indicate that this page will become a peer page of the home page. Release the mouse button.

3. Close the folder list. Here's what the structure looks like now:

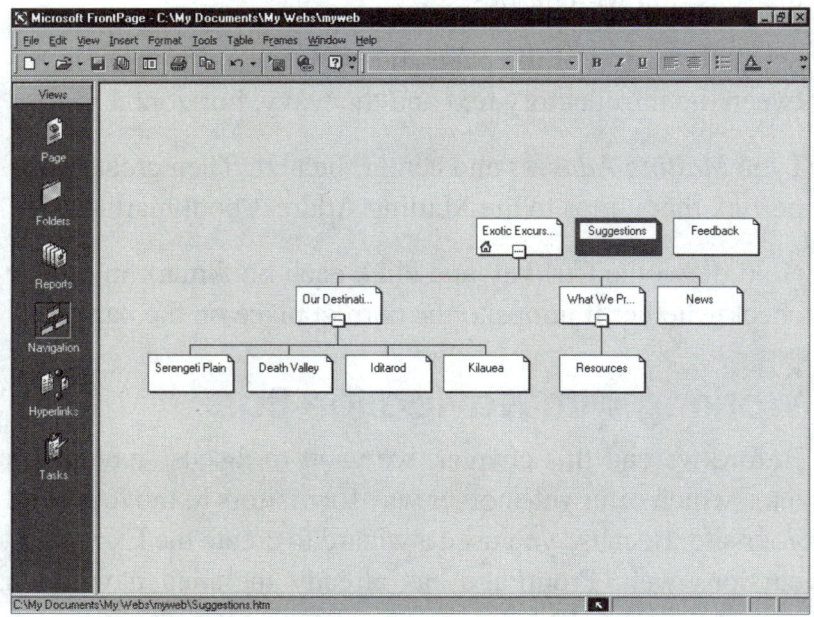

Adding navigation bars

To add a new navigation bar to a page, first click an insertion point where you want the navigation bar to appear. (If the insertion point is in a shared border, the new navigation bar will be added to all pages.) Next choose Navigation Bar from the Insert menu and then select the hyperlinks option you want for the navigation bar in the Hyperlinks To Add To Page section. In the Orientation And Appearance section, select either the Horizontal or Vertical option to determine the orientation of the navigation bar and select either Text or Buttons to determine the appearance. (The Buttons option works only if you have applied a theme to your web.) Then click OK.

4. Double-click the Exotic Excursions box to view it in page view and notice that FrontPage has updated the buttons in the top shared border.

Chapter 2 Enhancing Your Web

5. Test the new Suggestions button to see whether it moves you to the correct page. Notice that the Suggestions page now has a top navigation bar and a page banner title.

   Testing new navigation buttons

   That takes care of updating the web's navigation structure so that the top navigation bar includes all three top-level pages. Now you need to figure out how best to display the other levels so that you can access any page from any other page. Because the navigation bars appear in shared borders, any change you make on one page will be reflected on all the others. You need to come up with one scheme that will work for all the pages, which sometimes takes a little trial and error. Follow these steps:

1. Display the home page and notice that the navigation bar below the Exotic Excursions page banner doesn't contain any information. On this page, it would make sense to have buttons for the child pages of the home page appear here instead of in the navigation bar on the left.

2. Click the navigation bar placeholder below the banner to select it, right-click the selection, and choose Navigation Bar Properties from the shortcut menu to display this dialog box:

   Changing navigation bar buttons

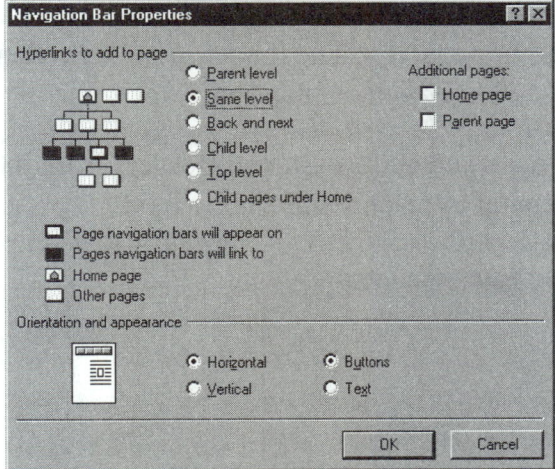

Reformatting navigation bars

To change the formatting of a navigation bar when you haven't applied a theme, select the navigation bar and make changes to the font size, type, or color in the usual way. If you have applied a theme and want to reformat a navigation bar, you can either switch to another theme or modify the theme to your specifications (see the tip on page 42 for more information).

3. Click the Child Level option in the Hyperlinks To Add To Page section. Check that the options in the Additional Pages section are deselected, then check that the Horizontal and Buttons options in the Orientation And Appearance section are selected, and click OK. Now the same navigation buttons

appear in the navigation bar below the banner and the bar in the left shared border.

4. Display the Our Destinations page. The changes you have made to the top navigation bar and the bar below the banner work fine for this page, but you really need to be able to access the child pages of the home page from the bar on the left.

5. Click the left navigation bar to select it, right-click the selection, and choose Navigation Bar Properties. In the Hyperlinks To Add To Page section, click the Child Pages Under Home option. Next check that the Additional Pages options are deselected and that the Vertical and Buttons options in the Orientation And Appearance section are selected. Click OK. Now you have access to all your web's pages from this page.

6. Go ahead and flip through all the pages using the Ctrl+click method to verify that the navigation bars are now set up correctly. Buttons for Home, Suggestions, and Feedback should appear at the top of each page; each page's child pages (if any) should appear on the bar below the banner; and buttons for the home page's child pages should appear on the left bar.

This system works for all but the home page, which has duplicate buttons. But if you change the button configuration of the left bar to suit the home page, it will no longer suit all the other pages. Here's how to remedy the situation:

1. Display the home page and choose Shared Borders from the expanded Format menu to display this dialog box:

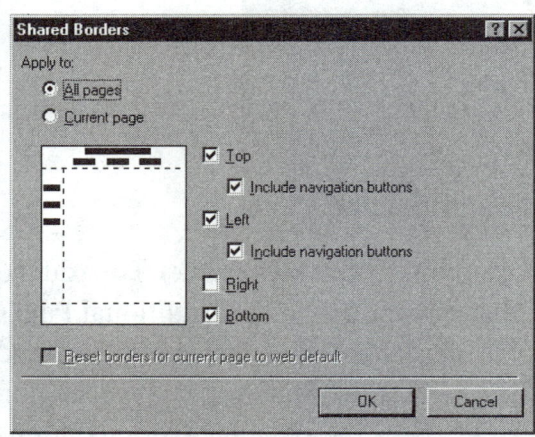

Changing the default button names

By default, FrontPage uses the names *Home*, *Up*, *Back*, and *Next* for its standard navigation buttons. If you want to change these names, you can do so by choosing Web Settings from the Tools menu and displaying the Navigation tab. Then type a new name in the appropriate edit box and click OK. To restore the default settings, display the dialog box again and click the Default button.

2. Select the Current Page option to turn off the shared border on this page only. Then click the Left check box to deselect it and click OK. Here are the results:

Turning off shared borders on one page only

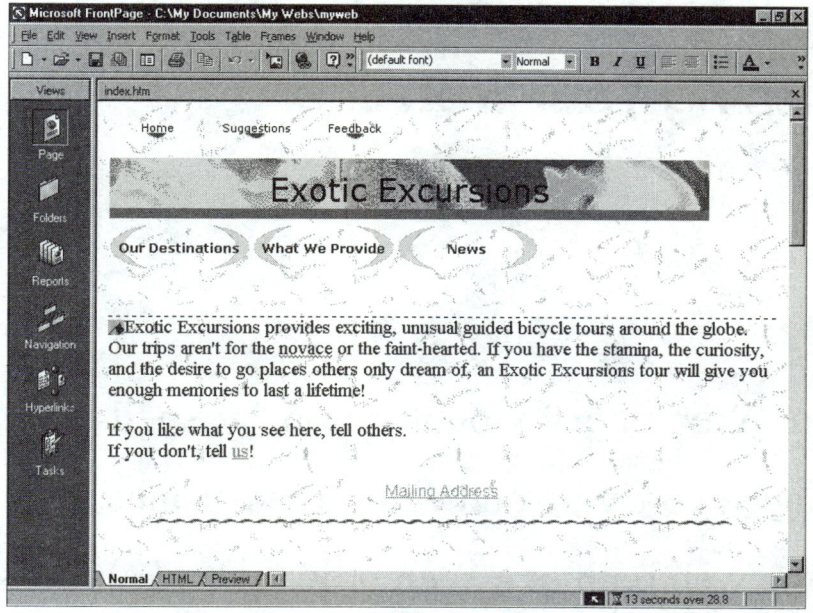

3. Display each page in turn to verify that the navigation bars work for all pages.

4. Save all your work. (On the Window menu, any page with unsaved changes is marked by an asterisk. Simply display that page and click the Save button.) Then quit FrontPage.

Now that you have added some graphics, applied a theme, and created and edited hyperlinks throughout your web, you are ready to prepare for final publishing on the World Wide Web. We'll take you through that process in the next chapter.

3
Publishing Your Web Site

You prepare your Web site for publication by spell-checking your pages, verifying and editing hyperlinks, and previewing the web both in a Web browser and on paper. We then discuss how to find a Web Presence Provider and how to send your files to a server.

By working through this chapter with a sample web, you acquire the skills necessary to publish your own webs, whether you are posting pages of information for your organization, for customers, or for friends and family.

Tasks performed and concepts covered:

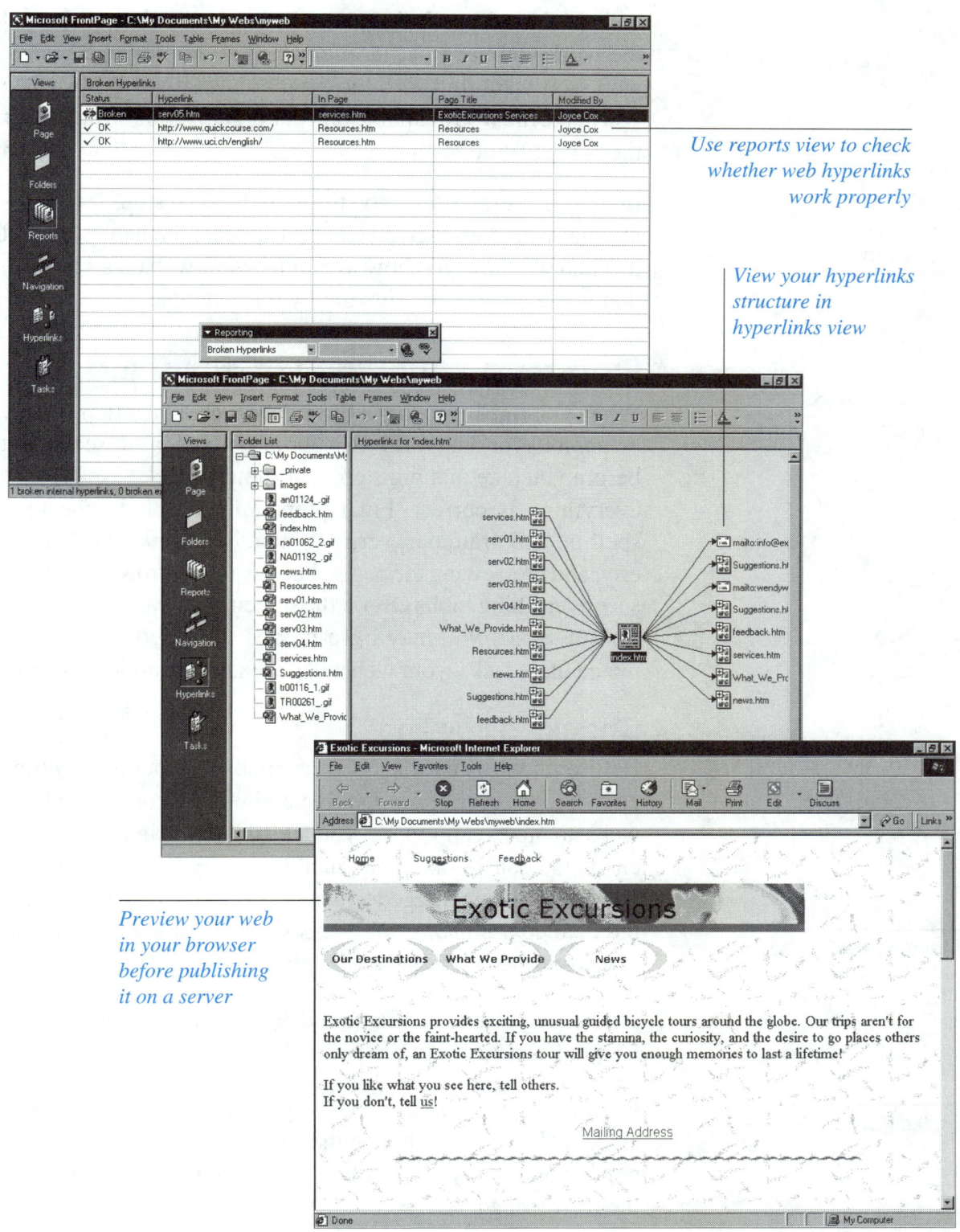

Use reports view to check whether web hyperlinks work properly

View your hyperlinks structure in hyperlinks view

Preview your web in your browser before publishing it on a server

In the first two chapters, you created a web for Exotic Excursions, a fictitious bike tour company. In the process, you learned how to enter and fine-tune text, as well as add graphics, hyperlinks, and other special effects. After all the work you have put in to create this simple yet effective web, you want things to look right and run smoothly when you make the web available on your organization's intranet or the World Wide Web.

In this chapter, we take you through the final steps for ensuring that your web is error-free and appears the way you want it. Then we show you how to publish your web on a server so that it is available for viewing by other people.

Preparing Your Web for Publishing

When you finish creating a FrontPage web, you will probably be anxious for the world (or your organization) to see it. But before you take that big step, you should check to make sure everything is correct. Final preparations include checking spelling and grammar, verifying that hyperlinks work properly, and previewing the pages, both in a Web browser to make sure everything looks OK on the screen and on paper to check for any errors you may have missed. Once you have completed these tasks, your web will be ready for public viewing.

Checking Spelling

Before making any document available for public scrutiny, you should check it for spelling and other errors. FrontPage webs are no exception. As you added the text in the previous chapters, you deliberately included a few errors, most of which FrontPage flagged with red, wavy underlines. This feature, called *automatic spell-checking*, alerts you to errors as you work. Let's fix one of the misspelled words now:

Automatic spell-checking

1. If necessary, start FrontPage and display the home page of the Exotic Excursions web.

Checking a word

2. Point to the word *novace* in the opening paragraph and right-click it. FrontPage checks the underlined word against its built-in dictionary and displays the shortcut menu at the top of the facing page.

Chapter 3 Publishing Your Web Site

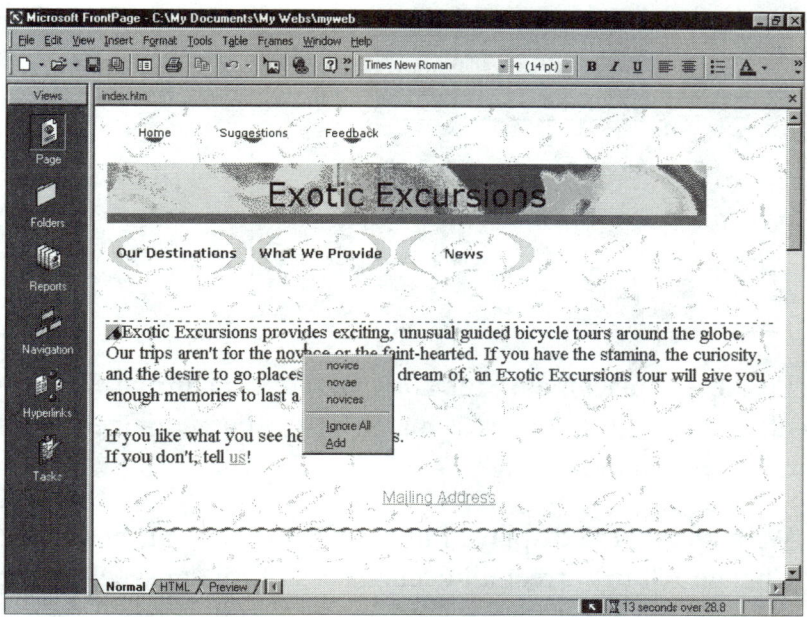

At the top of the shortcut menu, FrontPage displays any words in its dictionary that resemble the misspelled word. You can replace the underlined word with one of FrontPage's suggestions, ignore all instances of the misspelling, or add the underlined word to FrontPage's dictionary so that the program will recognize the word in the future.

3. Choose *novice* from the shortcut menu to replace the word with its correct spelling. The red, wavy underline disappears.

Checking the Spelling of an Entire Page

Right-clicking words with red, wavy underlines works well while you are entering text because you can take care of misspellings as they occur. But when you have finished work on a particular page, it's a good idea to check its spelling again. Follow these steps to check the entire home page:

1. With the home page displayed in page view, click the Spelling button on the Standard toolbar. FrontPage checks each word in the displayed page against its built-in dictionary, starting with the word containing the insertion point. When it finds a word that is not in its dictionary, it highlights the word and displays the dialog box shown on the next page.

The Spelling button

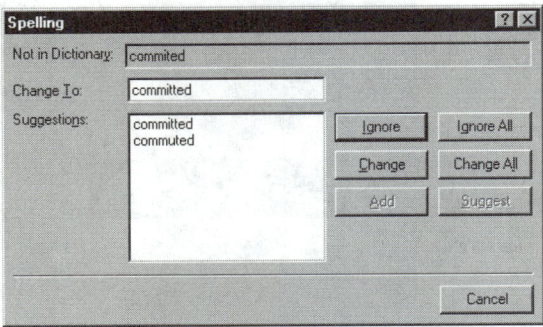

Possible replacements for *commited* appear in the Suggestions list, with the closest match to the unrecognized word displayed in the Change To edit box.

2. With *committed* displayed in the Change To edit box, click Change All to correct all occurrences of this misspelling on the page.

3. FrontPage stops at *beuty*. With *beauty* selected in the Change To box, click Change.

4. When FrontPage finishes checking the page, it closes the Spelling dialog box and displays a message stating that the spelling check is complete. Click OK.

5. Save the page.

Checking the Spelling of Multiple Pages

That spell check took care of the home page, but what about all the other pages? Here's how to check the spelling of the entire web:

1. Switch to navigation view and then click the Spelling button. (You can also check the spelling of the entire web in folders view.) FrontPage displays this dialog box:

2. With the Entire Web option selected, click Start to begin the spell check. After all the pages have been checked, you see

---

Spelling dictionaries

FrontPage checks your spelling by comparing each word in a web page to those in its built-in dictionary and in a supplemental dictionary called Custom.dic. If a word is not in either dictionary, FrontPage displays the Spelling dialog box and awaits your instructions. Though you can't edit the built-in dictionary, you can add words to Custom.dic by clicking the Add button in the Spelling dialog box. See the adjacent page for specific steps.

this dialog box, where FrontPage lists any potential misspellings it found:

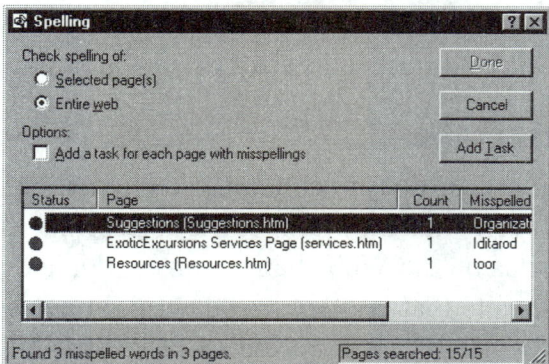

Here you can scan the list of misspellings and then move to the appropriate page in page view to fix a problem. You can also select an item from the list and click the Add Task button to add a reminder to fix that problem to the tasks list. Or you can click the Add A Task check box under Options to add a task for each of the pages that have problems.

Adding spelling problems to the tasks list

3. Double-click the first entry (the one on the Suggestions page). FrontPage opens that page in page view and displays the Spelling dialog box shown on the facing page with the potential misspelling identified.

4. This misspelling is a placeholder name that you have not yet replaced. Change the entry in the Change To box to *Exotic Excursions* and click Change.

5. When FrontPage asks if you want to move to the next document with a misspelling, click the Next Document button.

6. FrontPage stops on *Iditarod* on the Services (Our Destinations) page. You have spelled this name correctly and use it often. To prevent FrontPage from flagging it as a misspelling every time, add it to the supplemental dictionary, Custom.dic, by clicking the Add button. (You cannot add words to the main dictionary.) Then click Next Document.

Adding words to the dictionary

7. With *tour* selected in the Change To box, click Change.

8. When FrontPage finishes the spell check, click OK in the message box and click Cancel to close the Spelling dialog box.

Proofreading

9. Because errors of syntax or improper word usage can easily slip by, you can't rely on FrontPage's spelling checker to identify every error in your web pages. The home page of the Exotic Excursions web contains such an error. Read through all the text on that page and correct the error when you find it.

Checking Hyperlinks

The Exotic Excursions web doesn't contain many hyperlinks, but you should still verify that they jump to the correct places. Bear in mind that sites on the Web change constantly, and a hyperlink to another site that is correct today might not be correct tomorrow. To check your hyperlinks, you will explore two more FrontPage views: hyperlinks view and reports view.

Checking in Hyperlinks View

Hyperlinks view gives you an overview of all the hyperlinks in a web, much the same as navigation view gives you an overview of the organization of a web's pages. Let's look at the Exotic Excursions web in hyperlinks view now. Follow these steps:

1. Display each page in turn and click the Save button to save all your changes.

The Hyperlinks icon

2. With the home page displayed, click the Hyperlinks icon on the Views bar to display your web like this:

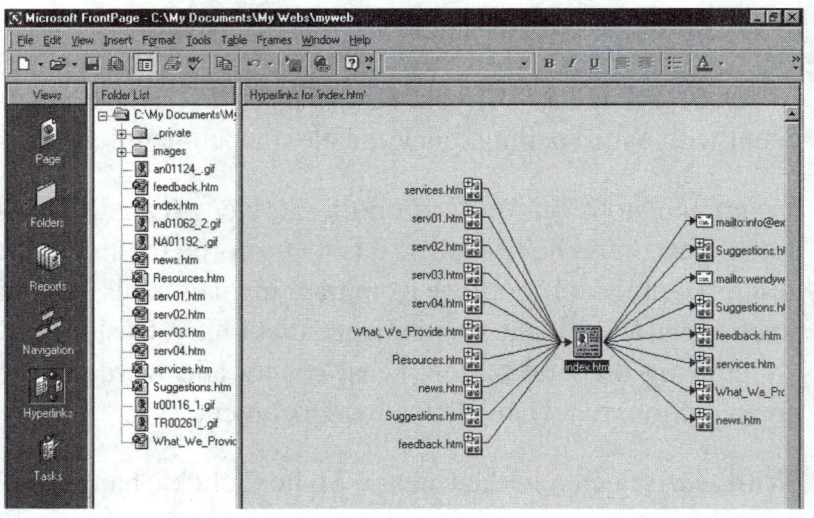

Icons in hyperlinks view

The icons you will see in hyperlinks view include an envelope, which represents an e-mail hyperlink; a page with a globe on it, which represents a link to the Web; and a picture icon, which represents a link to a graphic.

In the left pane is the folder list of all the pages in your web. In the right pane is a diagram with the home page (index.htm) in the middle and all the connected pages and hyperlinks displayed on either side. The arrows show how each page is connected. Links from the pages on the left are represented by the arrows to the home page. Links from the home page are represented by the arrows to the pages on the right.

3. Click the Folder List button on the toolbar to close the left pane. Then click the plus sign on the news.htm icon on the right side of the home page icon to display the hyperlinks for the News page, as shown below:

Expanding the diagram

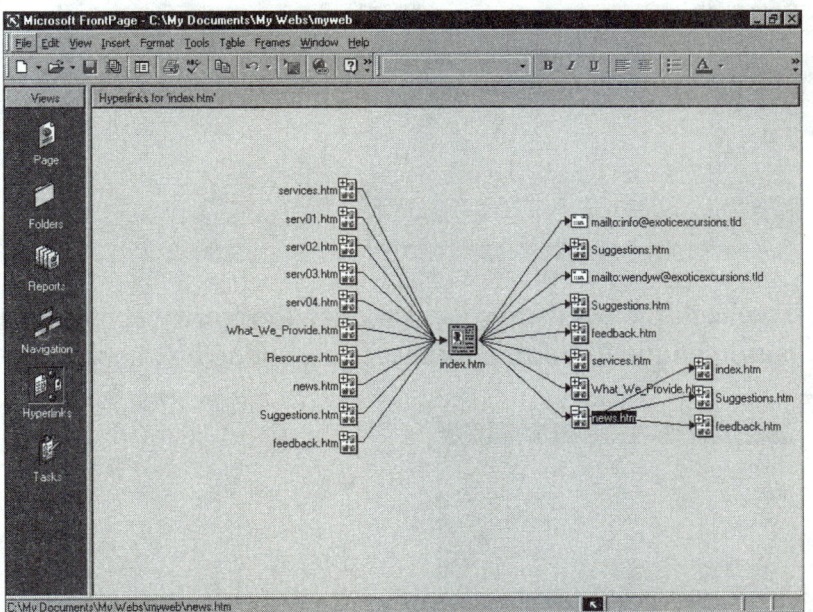

4. Click the minus sign to collapse the News page's hyperlinks.

Collapsing the diagram

Checking in Reports View

As you just saw, hyperlinks view is helpful for looking over the layout of your hyperlinks, but it doesn't tell you whether they are all working correctly. To check whether all the hyperlinks in a web are functional, you use reports view. Follow the steps on the next page.

The Reports icon

1. Click the Reports icon on the Views bar. Your screen looks like the one shown below. (We dragged the Reporting toolbar out of the way so that it doesn't obscure the files list.)

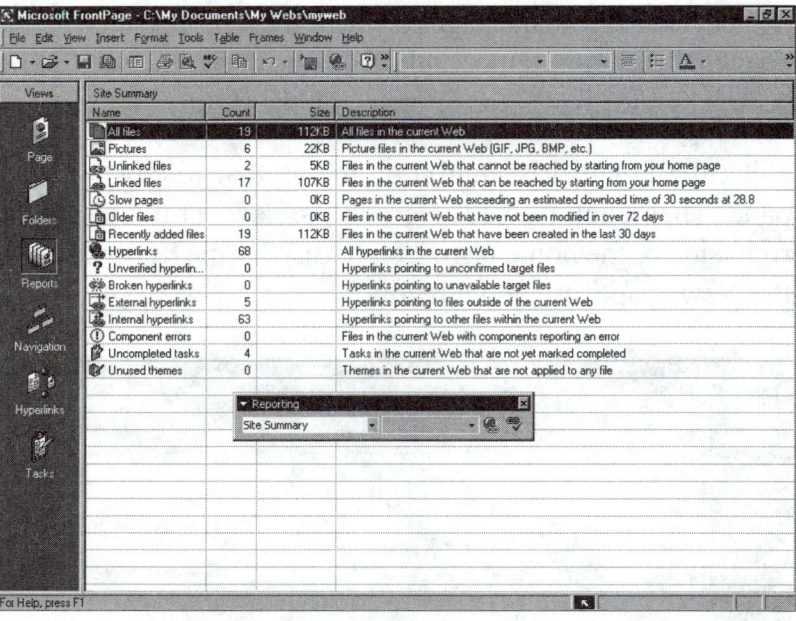

The Verify Hyperlinks button

2. To check the web's hyperlinks, click the Verify Hyperlinks button on the Reporting toolbar. This dialog box appears:

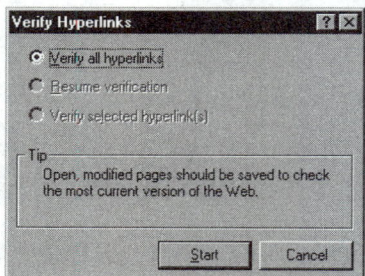

3. Check that the Verify All Hyperlinks option is selected and then click Start. If one or more of the hyperlinks is to a site on the Web, you may be prompted to connect to the Internet. FrontPage then very quickly tests any links that haven't already been verified. When it completes the test, your screen looks as shown at the top of the facing page.

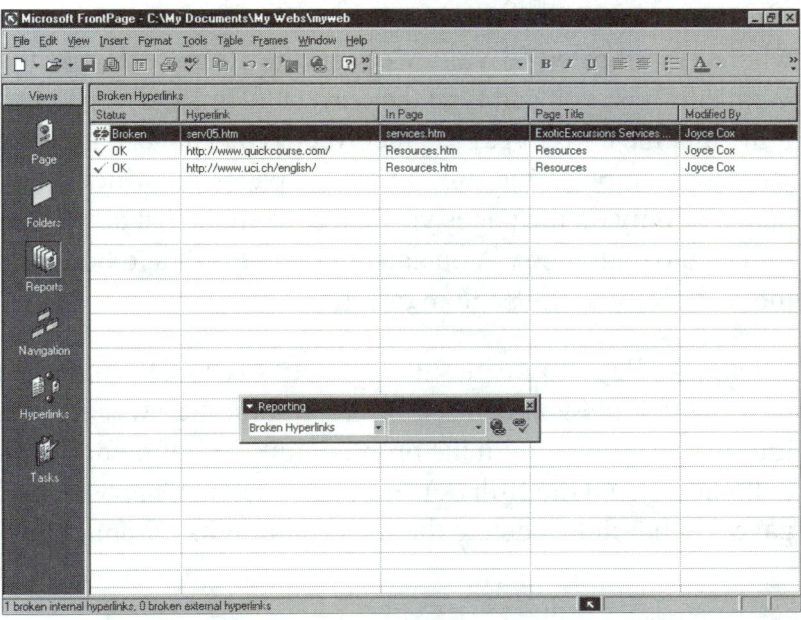

4. If necessary, disconnect from the Internet.

Editing Hyperlinks

If you are fortunate, you will see no Broken symbols in the Status column. However, when problems do occur, you need to know how to edit a hyperlink. Follow these steps:

1. Right-click the broken serv05.htm hyperlink and choose Edit Hyperlink from the shortcut menu. FrontPage displays this dialog box:

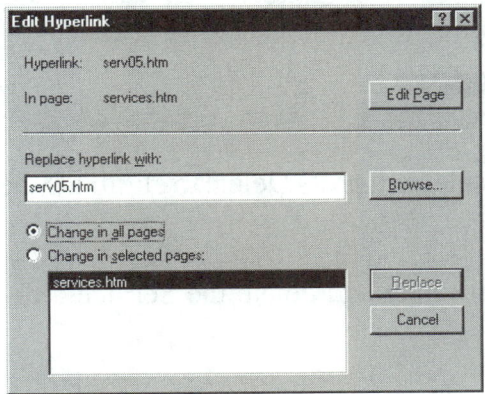

Other reports views

You can change the reports view by clicking the arrow to the right of the Report box on the Reporting toolbar and making a selection from the drop-down list. You can create reports that include all recently added files, recently changed files, slow pages, pages with component errors, and so on. With some report types, you can change the option in the Report Setting drop-down list to fine-tune the report even further. You can also change how FrontPage determines certain report settings, such as what constitutes "recent" or "slow." Choose Options from the Tools menu and display the Reports View tab. Then change the default settings in the appropriate edit boxes and click OK.

Editing hyperlinks

The Edit Hyperlink dialog box shows the name of the link and where it is located in your web. In the Replace Hyperlink With edit box, you can type the correct address, if you determine that the current page is incorrect. You can also indicate whether to replace the link on all the pages on which it appears, or only on the pages you select from the list at the bottom of the dialog box. You can click the Edit Page button to move directly to the page in question.

2. Click Edit Page to display the Services (Our Destinations) page, which (as you can see in the graphic below) includes links to child pages with the problem link highlighted. Recall that you deleted the fifth Service page back in Chapter 1 (see page 17) but didn't delete the hyperlink on its parent page.

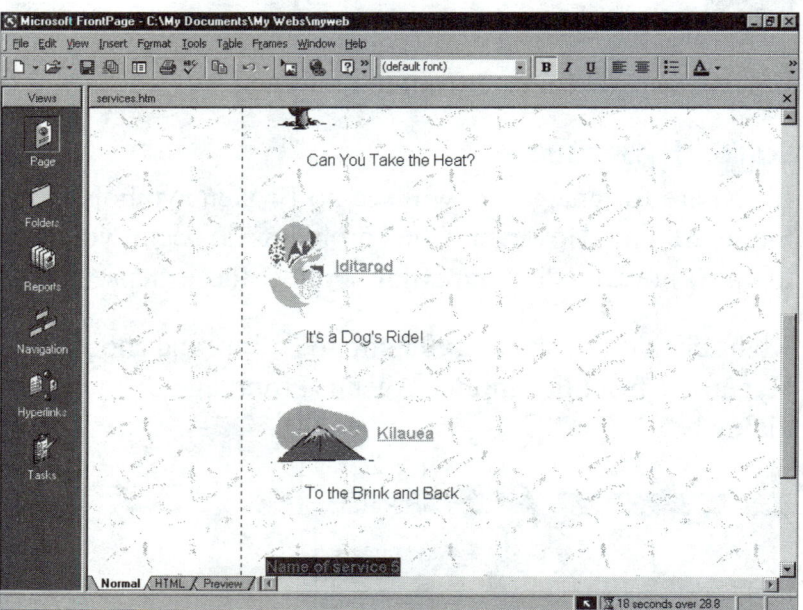

3. With *Name of Service 5* selected, press Delete to eliminate the problem.

4. Scroll the page and then select and delete the Service 5 description.

Previewing a Web

One of the final steps in preparing your web for publication is to preview it, checking the placement of items on the pages, color schemes, legibility of the text against the background, and so on. With FrontPage, you have two ways to preview your web: on the Preview tab and in a Web browser.

You have already used the page view's Preview tab a few times to examine your pages. This method is handy because it is easily accessible, but the Preview tab doesn't always render your web pages accurately. It is best, and nearly as easy, to preview your pages using your Web browser before exposing them to other people's scrutiny. For this example, you will use Internet Explorer, but if possible, you should check your web in other browsers as well, so that you can detect any design problems that might arise because of browser differences. Follow these steps to preview your web:

1. Display the Exotic Excursions home page in page view and click the Save button to save any outstanding changes.

2. Click the Preview In Browser button on the Standard toolbar. Your screen now looks something like the one shown here:

The Preview In Browser button

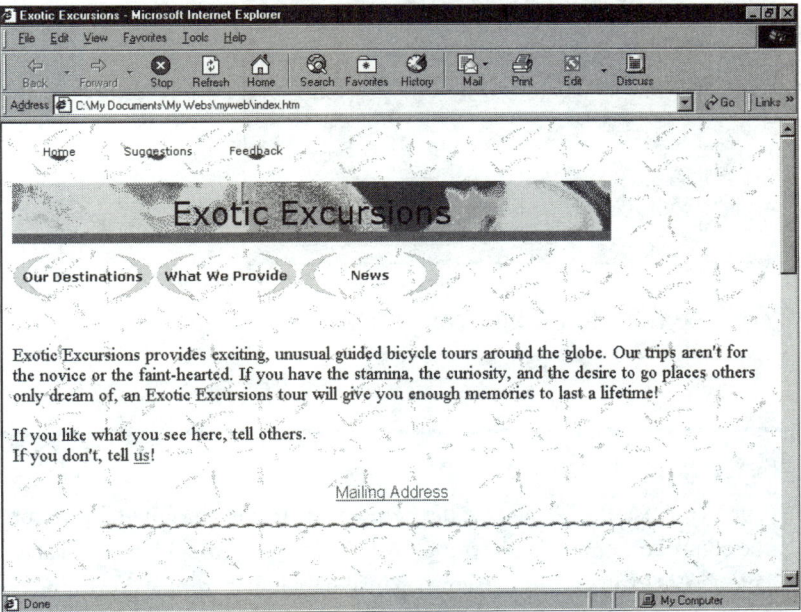

3. Test the various hyperlinks on your web's pages to verify that they move you to the correct locations. (If you click an external hyperlink, you may be prompted to connect to the Internet.)

Browser-specific webs

If your organization has standardized on a particular browser and you are publishing on an intranet, you can tell FrontPage to use features that will work only in that browser (or a specific version of that browser). Choose Page Options from the Tools menu, click the Compatibility tab, and make the selections you want from the Browsers, Browser Versions, and Servers drop-down lists. FrontPage then shows you which of its features you can use in the Technologies section of the dialog box.

4. When you are finished testing, close the browser window and, if necessary, disconnect from the Internet.

Printing a Web

Another optional final step involves printing the pages of your web so that you can proofread them on paper. It's surprising how many errors missed during on-screen editing are found when you read a printout. Follow these steps:

The Print button

1. Move to the What We Provide page in page view and click the Print button on the Standard toolbar. FrontPage prints one copy of What_We_Provide.htm.

2. Now display the home page and choose Print from the File menu. FrontPage displays a dialog box like this one:

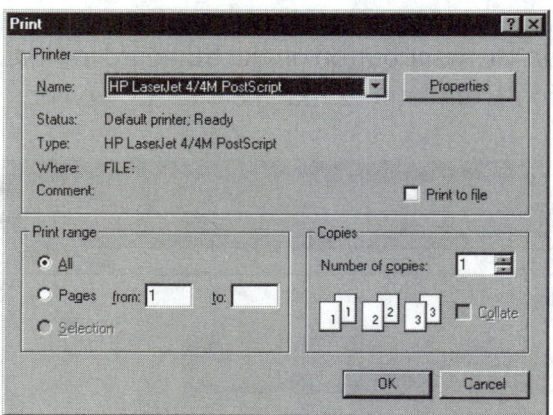

(You see the dialog box for your default printer.)

More print options

To "print" an image of the page to a file on disk, click the Print To File check box. Clicking the Properties button displays a dialog box with additional options, including page orientation (Portrait vs. Landscape). You can also choose Page Setup from the File menu and select the orientation you want in the Print Setup dialog box.

Setting up for printing

When you installed Windows, the Setup program also installed the driver (the control program) for the printer attached to your computer. If you also have access to other printers, you can install their drivers by using the Add Printer Wizard in the Printers folder. (Choose Settings and then Printers from the Start menu.) FrontPage can access all the installed printers, but only one at a time. In the Print dialog box, click the arrow to the right of the Name box in the Printer section, select the printer you want to use, and then click OK.

If the page is fairly long, you can print parts of it—for example, just the first page—by clicking the Pages option in the Print Range section and then entering the page numbers in the From and To boxes. To print more than one copy, change the setting in the Number of Copies box in the Copies section.

← Printing parts of a page

3. To print one copy of the home page, simply click OK.

Publishing a Web

After investing so much time and energy in creating your web, you will want to be able to share it with other people by publishing it on a Web server. It then becomes a Web site that can be accessed and viewed using a Web browser. To publish your web, you need to know the address of the server you will use to host it. (There may be times when you might create the web on the computer that functions as the server.)

In the case of an intranet, the publishing process is pretty simple, and undoubtedly someone in your organization will be able to guide you. In the case of Internet publishing, things are a little more complex, so we'll briefly look at some of the issues here.

About FrontPage Server Extensions

In order for a FrontPage web to be fully functional as a Web site in a Web browser, the server that hosts the web should have the Microsoft FrontPage Server Extensions installed, regardless of whether the server is on the Internet or an intranet. These extensions are a set of programs that enable the Webmaster to administer the site, authors to continue developing it, and visitors to browse it. The extensions can be installed on computers running most common Web-server packages, including those from Microsoft, Netscape, and Apache.

The FrontPage Server Extensions offer several advantages. Webmasters can determine who is allowed to administer, change, and view the Web site, by setting permissions for different types of users. As a result, they can maintain security on their systems. As the web's author, you can take advantage

Transfer protocols →

of such features as forms, hit counters, and the other components that can be added to a web (see Chapters 5 and 6). After the web is published, you can continue to create and update individual pages that have hyperlinks, navigation bars, and interactive elements. You can also create documents with the programs that are part of the Microsoft Office 2000 suite and save them as part of the Web site. The extensions make sure the integrity of the site is not compromised by these updates and additions. You can continue using FrontPage to manage your web as it evolves, ensuring that the version on your computer and the version on the server stay in sync. In addition, the extensions allow you to transfer your files to your Web server using the HyperText Transfer Protocol (HTTP). If the Web server doesn't have the extensions, you must use File Transfer Protocol (FTP); see FrontPage's Help feature for more information.

With all these advantages, before you publish your web, you will want to make sure the Web server you'll use supports the FrontPage Server Extensions.

Finding a Web Presence Provider

If you already have an Internet Service Provider (ISP), your best bet is to contact them either by phone or e-mail and ask whether they will host your Web site and whether they can support a site created with FrontPage 2000. If they can't, you will probably want to locate a provider that can. (In FrontPage terminology, organizations that own Web servers equipped with the FrontPage Server Extensions are called *Web Presence Providers*, or *WPPs*.)

No extensions?
If you know that the Web server you will use does not support the FrontPage Server Extensions, you can choose Page Options from the Tools menu, click the Compatibility tab, deselect the Enabled With Microsoft FrontPage Server Extensions check box, and click OK. Any features that require these extensions will then be unavailable.

FrontPage can assist you in locating a provider that has the necessary extensions installed on its server so that all FrontPage features will run properly. Let's try locating one now, by following these steps:

1. With the home page displayed in page view, choose Publish Web from the File menu. FrontPage displays this dialog box:

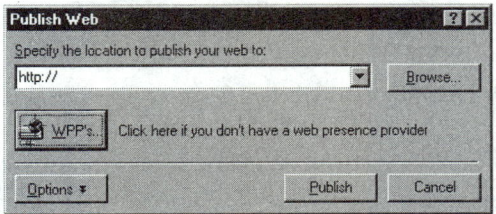

2. Click the WPP's button to begin the procedure for locating a provider.

3. Your Web browser starts and may prompt you to connect to the Internet. You then move to a page on Microsoft's Web site that lists some of the larger WPPs and also has a hyperlink to other pages about FrontPage.

4. Browse through the WPP list alphabetically or geographically. You might find your current ISP in one of these lists, or you might locate a new one in your area.

5. After you finish exploring the WPP list and related pages and have the information you need, close your Web browser and disconnect from the Internet if necessary.

6. Back in FrontPage, click Cancel to close the Publish Web dialog box.

You can now contact the WPP and if necessary, establish an account that enables you to publish your own Web site.

Sending a Web to a Server

The next step in publishing a web is to send it to your Web server. The procedure for sending your web files, also called *uploading*, is made quite simple with the help of the Microsoft Web Publishing Wizard, but you will still need to obtain specific instructions from your WPP. The general procedure is as follows:

◀ **The Microsoft Web Publishing Wizard**

1. With your web open in page view, choose Publish Web from the File menu to display the dialog box shown at the top of this page.

2. In the Specify The Location To Publish Your Web To edit box, enter the URL for your Web server and click Publish. Then connect to the Internet if prompted.

3. When the Microsoft Web Publishing Wizard asks for a user name and password, enter the name and password you were given by your WPP and then click Finish. FrontPage then begins transferring your web files to the server.

4. If you see a Publishing FrontPage Components dialog box, click Continue to display a dialog box that tracks the progress of the file transfer from your computer to the server.

After FrontPage completes the transfer, the only thing left to do is check your site on the Web by following these steps:

Testing your Web site

1. Start your Web browser. (If prompted, connect to the Internet.)

2. Type the URL you received from your WPP in the Address bar and press Enter. (This URL will probably consist of the Web server's URL followed by a slash, and might include a directory name or two, another slash, and then the filename of your web's home page, index.htm.)

3. Once the home page is displayed, you can move among the various pages by clicking the text hyperlinks and the buttons on the navigation bars. You might also want to try sending yourself an e-mail message to make sure that the line of communication with your viewers is open.

Deleting a FrontPage Web

After practicing with FrontPage, you will probably end up with a web that you no longer need. It's not wise to delete the web using normal Windows techniques because of all the associated files that FrontPage created behind the scenes. However, deleting a FrontPage web is not difficult. If you are continuing on to Part Two of this book, you don't want to delete the web you have created by following our example yet. But when you're ready, here are the steps:

1. Open the web you want to delete and display the folder list.

2. Right-click the web's folder at the top of the folder list and choose Delete from the shortcut menu. FrontPage warns you that deletion of a web is a permanent action and offers you the two choices shown here:

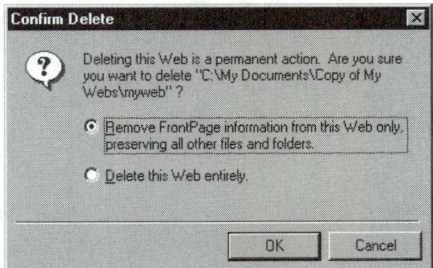

You can remove only the FrontPage information, leaving intact any files you have used in your web pages, such as text files or graphics; or you can remove the web in its entirety.

3. Click the option you want and then click OK. Otherwise, click Cancel.

Having completed Part One of this Quick Course, you are now equipped to produce and publish simple webs that will meet most of your needs. In Part Two, we explore techniques for creating more complex webs.

PART TWO

BUILDING PROFICIENCY

You build on the techniques you learned in Part One to create more sophisticated web pages. After completing these chapters, you will be able to develop Web sites that effectively communicate your message. In Chapter 4, you display information in a frames page and a table, and gather information via an input form. In Chapter 5, you add special effects such as hotspots, hover buttons, and sound to your pages. In Chapter 6, you learn various ways to maintain and update your web site so that the information displayed is always current.

4
Creating a More Complex Web

In this chapter, you take a look at some of the more complex elements you can add to a web. First you create a new web so that you can experiment with a frames page. Next you insert and format a table. Finally, you work with forms.

These elements are prevalent in many business-related Web sites. However, the techniques you learn can easily be applied to webs for other types of organizations, as well as personal webs.

Web pages created and concepts covered:

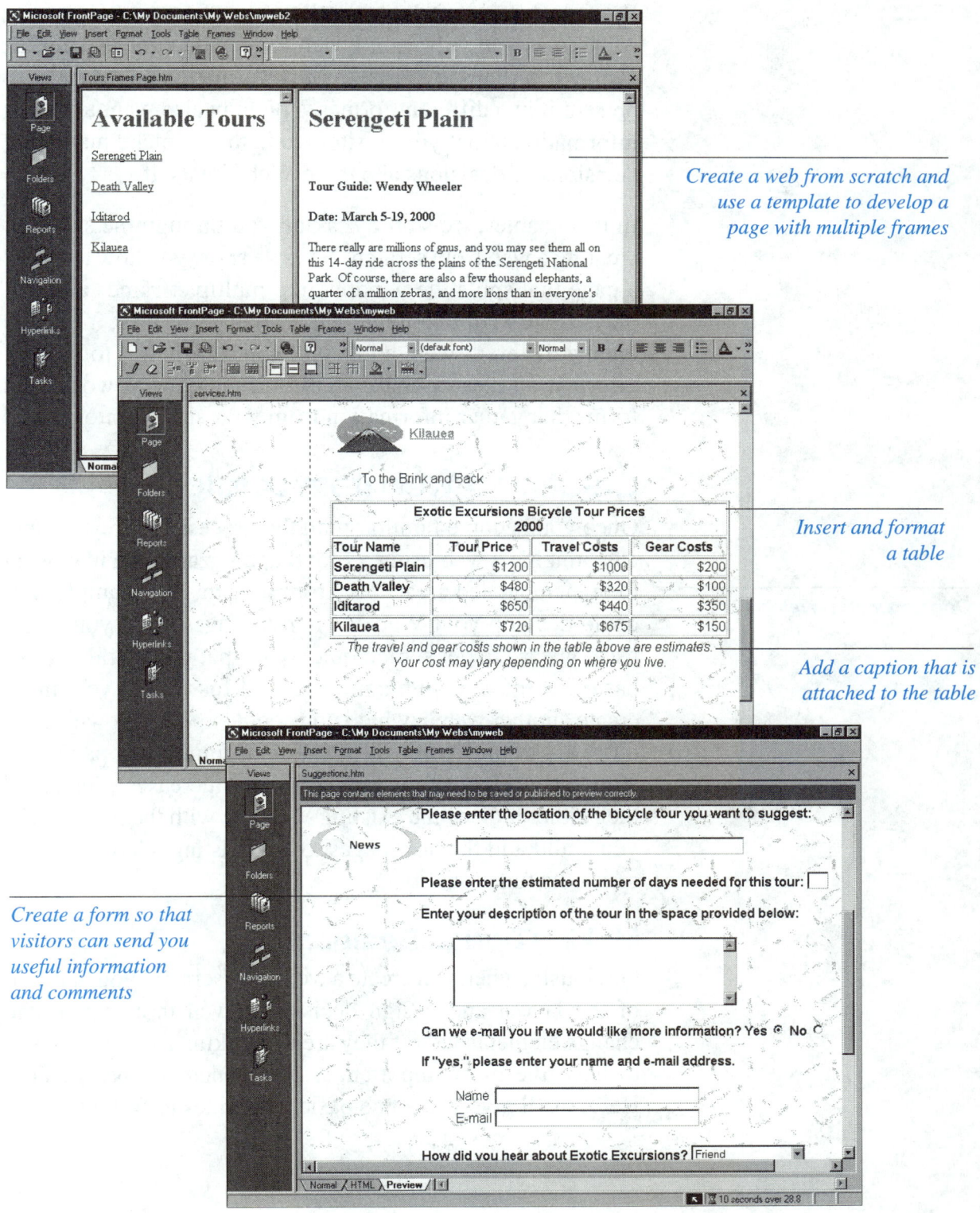

Create a web from scratch and use a template to develop a page with multiple frames

Insert and format a table

Add a caption that is attached to the table

Create a form so that visitors can send you useful information and comments

In Part One, you started developing the basic components for a simple, yet effective web for Exotic Excursions. By using a wizard and applying a theme, you allowed FrontPage to take care of a lot of the design work for you. However, sometimes you will want a web to include a more complex element, perhaps to present more information on a page or to present it in a different format. You may also want to gather information about your visitors to help you make marketing decisions or decisions about the Web site itself.

In this chapter, we start by taking you through the steps for creating a web from scratch. Next we show you how to create a page that splits the window into multiple frames and displays more than one item of information at once. You then open a different web, add a table, and format it to present information clearly and concisely. Finally, you work with forms that gather information from your site's visitors.

Creating a Web from Scratch

Once you become familiar with the process for creating and customizing a web using a FrontPage wizard, you may want to branch out and create one from scratch. For example, you could develop your Web site in two stages. First you might use a wizard to get started quickly so that you could publish basic information with a minimum of fuss. Then you might create another web in which you could experiment with various ways of presenting information, refining your pages and adding new elements as your skill level increases. You could then either replace the existing Web site with the new one, or you could add the new pages to the existing Web site to increase its functionality.

Ongoing web development

Making Design Decisions

Obviously, when you create a web from scratch, you make all of the layout and design decisions. Even though you can change elements later if they aren't working for you, it's best to have the most important issues ironed out beforehand. Here, we'll give you some basic guidelines to follow.

Defining the Target Audience

You need to determine the type of audience you are trying to attract so that you can make decisions about the tone, language level, and graphics you will use. Ask yourself these questions:

- **How old are they?** The answer to this question influences the reading level and language of your web, but it is also a major consideration when you are determining how you want the pages to look.

- **Does what you offer meet a need or satisfy a desire?** The answer to this question determines whether your design and tone are straightforward and down-to-earth, or exciting and evocative.

- **Do they have common interests, opinions, hopes, or fears?** The answer to this question influences the topics you address in your web and how you discuss them. If you don't know the answer and you want to appeal to the broadest possible audience, you'll want to keep your message general and steer clear of controversial topics.

- **What do they already know about this topic?** This question has two parts: what do they know in general, and what do they know about your organization, service, or product in particular? The answer to this question has some bearing on the amount of space you will dedicate to background information and whether you can use jargon.

Defining the Content

You need to decide what information you want to include and which elements are most important. To get a handle on how you will organize all this information, ask yourself the following questions:

- **What information needs to be presented?** The beauty of a web is that you can throw in everything that you think might be of even remote interest to your audience. But such a sprawling web takes time to implement in a meaningful way, and perhaps more important, time to maintain.

Generating traffic

If you are creating a Web site to promote your product or service, or even your point of view, your efforts will be wasted if nobody ever looks at the site. One of the ways to ensure that people will find your site is to register with the major search services, such as Yahoo and AltaVista. (You'll find information on their Web sites about this process.) Once that step is complete, you will most likely start to get e-mail messages offering, for a fee, to register your site with a hundred or more other Web databases. Another step you can take is to include in your site HTML codes called meta tags. These tags are used by programs called Web crawlers to compile databases of the information available on the web. The tags are placed at the top of your web site's home page and contain keywords that describe what your site is about. (See FrontPage's Help feature for more information about meta tags.)

- **How will you organize the information?** The answer to this question will depend a lot on the web's purpose. If you are creating a web to promote a product to the outside world, your information will likely be organized very differently than if you are creating an informational intranet for your organization's employees.

- **What information needs to be most accessible?** When deciding on your information's hierarchy, you need to place the content that is likely to be needed most often no more than one click away from the home page. Yet you don't want the home page to become so cluttered that people can't easily find what they want.

- **What graphics are appropriate for your message?** If you have graphics available, determine which ones best enhance your message and fulfill the goals of your web.

By answering these and any other questions you can think of about your information and how your audience might want to use it, you can focus your efforts so that your web achieves the maximum results.

Starting an Empty Web

Suppose you want to experiment with presenting the Exotic Excursions tour information in a different format, but you don't want to risk messing up the Exotic Excursions web you created in Part One. In this section, we'll show you how to set up a new web so that you can play around with the pages that describe the available tours. Follow these steps:

1. If necessary, start FrontPage.

2. Choose New and then Web from the File menu to display the dialog box shown earlier on page 11.

3. Click the Empty Web icon. In the Options section, click an insertion point in the Specify The Location edit box and press End. Check that C:\My Documents\My Webs\myweb2 is specified as the location for the new web's folder, and click OK. FrontPage creates the new folder and displays a blank page called new_page_1.htm.

New dialog box options

If you want your web to have a more descriptive folder name than the generic Myweb, you can replace the name at the end of the path in the Specify The Location edit box. FrontPage then creates a folder with the name you enter. If you have already created a web and you now want to add pages to it, you can click one of the icons in the Web Sites list, select the name of the existing web from the Specify The Location drop-down list, and then click the Add To Current Web check box. For example, you might want to add Customer Support web pages to the Exotic Excursions web.

4. Close the folder list. Then with the insertion point located at the top of the new page, type *Serengeti Plain* and press Enter.

5. Select the text and format it as 6 (24 pt), bold, and green.

6. Press Ctrl+End to move to the blank paragraph below the heading and type the following text, pressing Enter once to start each new paragraph:

Tour Guide: Wendy Wheeler

Date: March 5-19, 2000

There really are millions of gnus, and you may see them all on this 14-day ride across the plains of the Serengeti National Park. Of course, there are also a few thousand elephants, a quarter of a million zebras, and more lions than in everyone's favorite animated movie. The terrain is fairly flat, but the climate in March is a bit of a challenge, with daytime temperatures of 95 degrees F.

7. Select the Tour Guide and Date lines and make them bold. Here are the results:

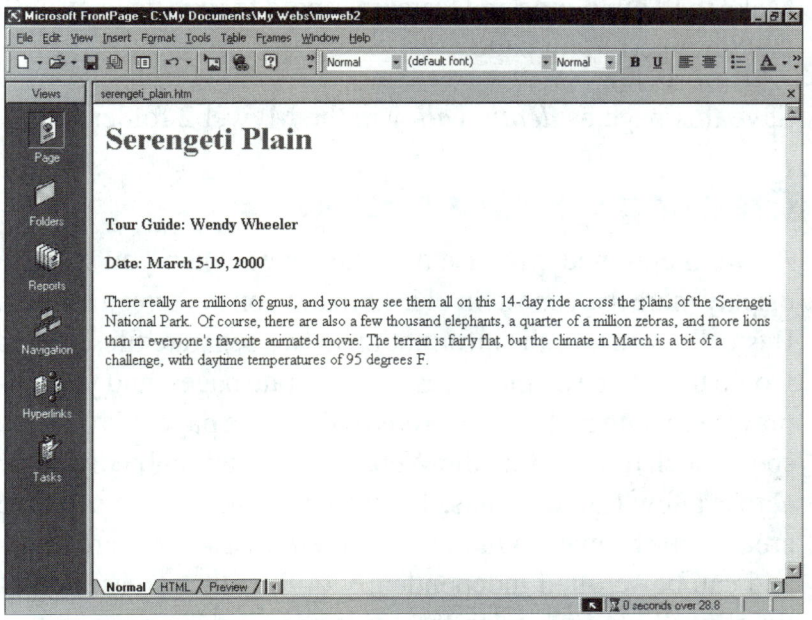

Importing existing files

When creating web pages in FrontPage, you may want to add an existing file created in another program as a page of your web. (You can also import an entire folder of files into your web.) To import an existing file into your web, first display the folder list and click the main web folder. (To import the file into a specific subfolder of your web, simply select the subfolder instead.) Choose Import from the File menu and click the Add File button. Then navigate to the storage location of the file you want to import, select it, and click Open. FrontPage adds the file to the list of available files in the web. (To import a folder, click Add Folder instead. To import a file from a different Web site, click the From Web button and then follow the instructions of the Import Web Wizard.) To quickly import a file stored on your hard drive, simply drag the file from Windows Explorer to the desired location in FrontPage's folder list.

Now you need to save the page as part of your new web:

1. Click the Save button to display the Save As dialog box.

2. Verify that the Myweb2 folder is displayed in the Save In box and that *serengeti_plain* is entered as the filename. Then click Save.

Now add a page about the Death Valley tour:

1. Click the New Page button, type *Death Valley*, and press Enter. Format the text to match the previous heading (see the previous page).

2. Next type the text shown below, pressing Enter to start new paragraphs:

   Tour Guide: Sandy Spokes

   Date: January 16-24, 2000

   One of the new rides we introduced in 1999, this January ride challenges your muscles and tests your stamina but rewards you with views of the California desert rarely seen by humans. The one thing you don't have to worry about is water. We supply lots of it to combat the only real obstacle on this truly scenic excursion.

3. Make the Tour Guide and Date lines bold for consistency with the Serengeti Plain page.

4. Save this page as *death_valley* in the Myweb2 folder.

Creating a Frames Page

As we mentioned, you use a frames page when you want to display more than one item of information on the screen at once. Basically, you take the information in two separate files, which would usually be displayed as two separate pages, and you display them both in different areas of the same page. If you have spent much time surfing the Web, you have undoubtedly come across a few frames pages. They are the ones where separate areas of the browser window have their own sets of scroll bars and can be scrolled independently of the other areas. Sometimes multiple frames on the same page can give the page a cluttered look. They can even be confusing. But used judiciously, frames pages can enable viewers to find the information they are looking for more conveniently and efficiently.

Scrolling frames independently

Using a Frames Page Template

Suppose you have decided that you want to list the available Exotic Excursions tours on one side of the page and be able to click a tour name in the list to display its details on the other side of the page. To develop such a setup, you need to create a new page using one of FrontPage's frames-page templates. Let's get started:

1. Choose New and then Page from the File menu and click the Frames Pages tab to display these options:

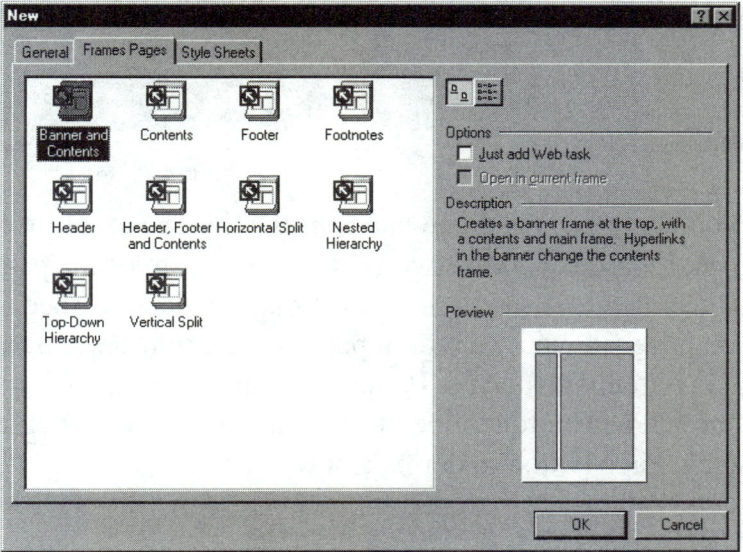

2. Click the icon for a frame type, read about that type in the Description section, and check out its layout in the Preview box. Then click other icons to see what's available.

Selecting a type

3. When you're ready, click the Contents icon and then click OK. Your screen now looks as shown on the next page.

> **Inserting a file in a page**
>
> If you have spent hours creating a document in Word or a spreadsheet in Excel that you want to insert in a page on your web, you can do so easily. To insert the file, click an insertion point where you want the file to appear and choose File from the Insert menu. Click the arrow to the right of the Files Of Type box and select the format of the file you want to insert. Then navigate to the file and double-click it. FrontPage converts the file to HTML format and incorporates it into the page as part of the page's file.

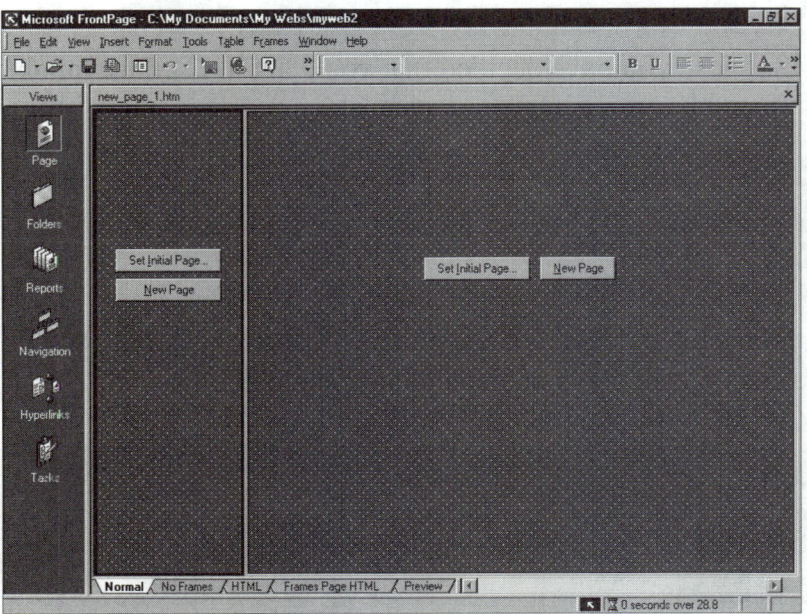

As you can see, FrontPage has split the new page into two frames. It has also added two tabs to the bottom of the page view window (see the tip below). You now need to specify which page file you want to appear in each frame when the page is initially displayed. For each frame, you can click the Set Initial Page button to specify an existing page file or click the New Page button to define a new page.

Setting Up the Contents Frame

The left frame will always display the same page. This page will function as the web's table of contents, but instead of being an actual table, the page will consist of a set of hyperlinks to other pages. When you click a hyperlink in the contents frame, the main frame on the right will change to display the hyperlink's target page. Follow these steps to set up the contents frame:

1. Check that the left frame is selected (it should be surrounded by a blue border) and then click the New Page button to display a blank page in that frame.

2. With the insertion point located in the new page, type the text on the facing page, pressing Enter after each line.

Other frames views

Some older Web browsers do not display frames pages correctly. To see the message displayed when a frames page is accessed in such a browser, click the No Frames tab in page view. You can modify the message, as well as add other elements to the page just as you normally would. To edit the "no frames" message, click the Frames Page HTML tab. (The HTML tab shows the code for the selected page, not the message.)

Available Tours

Serengeti Plain

Death Valley

Iditarod

Kilauea

3. Format the first line as 6 (24 pt), bold, and green. (Don't worry that the text wraps to a second line. You'll fix that problem in a moment.) Here are the results so far:

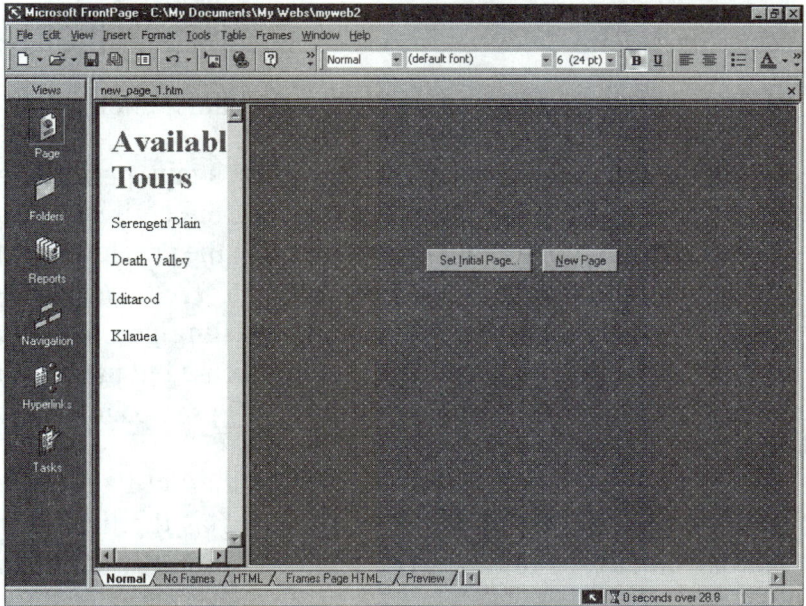

As with any other new page, after you create a new page as part of a frame, you need to save it. For you, the process is not much different from saving any page file. For FrontPage, however, things are a bit more complex. For a frames page, FrontPage creates separate files for the pages in the frames, as well as a file for the frames page itself. So if you have two frames, behind the scenes FrontPage will be juggling at least three files. Let's save the new page now:

1. With the new page selected, click the Save button on the toolbar to display the modified version of the Save As dialog box shown on the next page.

Saving the page

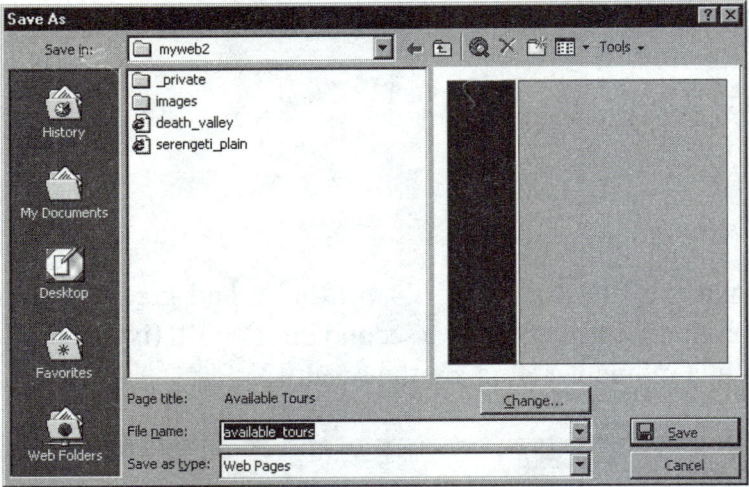

2. With *available_tours* specified as the filename, click Save.

Saving a frames page

3. FrontPage displays the Save As dialog box again, prompting you to save the frames page. (Notice that the entire frames page is surrounded by a thick blue border in the preview box.) Change the name in the File Name edit box to *Tours_Frames_Page*. (We will continue the practice of telling you to leave filenames specified by FrontPage all lowercase but use initial capital letters for the filenames you specify; see page 15.)

Giving a frames page a title

4. Next click the Change button to display the Set Page Title dialog box. Type *Exotic Excursions Tours* as the title your visitors should see in their Web browser's title bar and then click OK.

Setting Up the Main Frame

Now you can move on to the main frame on the right. Initially you want this frame to display the Serengeti Plain page you created earlier. Follow these steps:

Linking to the initial page

1. Click a blank area in the right frame to select it and then click the Set Initial Page button. FrontPage displays the Create Hyperlink dialog box shown earlier on page 44.

2. Select the Serengeti Plain page in the file list and click OK. FrontPage displays the page in the right frame.

3. Save your changes to the frames page.

Refining a Frames Page

Once you have specified which pages are to be displayed initially in a frames page, you can refine the page to make it function and look the way you want it. For the Exotic Excursion tours page, you first need to create the hyperlinks in the contents frame. Then visitors can display the description for a particular tour in the main frame by clicking its name in the contents frame. You also need to resize the contents frame, and the page could do with some formatting here and there.

Let's start with the easy stuff. Follow these steps to create links to the existing tour pages:

1. Select the *Serengeti Plain* heading in the contents frame, click the Hyperlink button on the toolbar, and double-click the Serengeti Plain file to create the hyperlink.

2. Repeat step 1 to create a hyperlink from the *Death Valley* heading to the Death Valley page.

3. Switch to the Preview tab and check that the hyperlinks are working correctly. Then switch back to the Normal tab.

Previewing the hyperlinks

Now create and link the two remaining tour pages:

1. Select the *Iditarod* heading, click the Hyperlink button, and click the Create A Page And Link To The New Page button. Then in the New dialog box, check that Normal Page is selected and click OK.

2. When FrontPage displays the new page, type the following:

Iditarod

Tour Guide: S.K. Moe

Date: July 17-25, 2000

This ride is our only mid-summer excursion. It follows the first third of the famous Iditarod Trail Sled Dog Race, from Anchorage to Nikolai, covering 350 miles in 6 days. Who needs the $50,000 prize money of the sled dog race? The rewards of this tour are spectacular views of the Alaskan wilderness and being able to show off the "I Did the Idit" t-shirt to your friends!

3. Format the heading as 6 (24 pt), bold, and green. Then make the Tour Guide and Date lines bold.

4. Save the new page as *iditarod*.

5. Choose Tours Frames Page from the Window menu to redisplay that page, and then repeat steps 1 through 4 to create a link to a new page called *kilauea*, using the information shown below to create the new page:

   Kilauea

   Tour Guide: Gary Gears

   Date: October 9-20, 2000

   Ride around one of the most spectacular geologic sites in the world. This 10-day trip on the island of Hawaii offers views of the Mauna Loa and Kilauea craters, as well as the many other splendors of the island. Along with steep rides up mountains, you will have to endure a tropical climate, afternoons at the beach, and plenty of leisure time to explore the largest of the Hawaiian islands.

6. Again, test your links on the Preview tab. As you move among the tour pages, check that their formatting is consistent. (You can return to the Normal tab to correct any problems you find.)

Now follow these steps to resize the contents frame so that its main heading is displayed on one line:

Resizing frames

1. Redisplay the Tours Frames Page and point to the dividing line between the two frames. When the pointer changes to a

---

Frame properties

To more precisely resize the windows of a frames page, select the frame you want to adjust and then choose Frame Properties from the Frames menu to display the Frame Properties dialog box. In the Frame Size section, enter a new width or height in the appropriate boxes. (You can set the size as a fixed number of pixels, or dots on the screen; as a percentage of the window's size; or relative to other frames in the same column.) You can also adjust the width and height of the frame's margins. To change the name of the frame, enter a new name in the Name box. To change the page initially displayed in the frame, click the Browse button and select a different file. In the Options section, select the Resizable In Browser check box if you want visitors to be able to resize the frame. You can also specify whether to display scrollbars in the frame only if needed, always, or never by selecting an option from the Show Scrollbars drop-down list.

double-headed arrow, drag to the right until the *Available Tours* heading appears on one line. Here are the results:

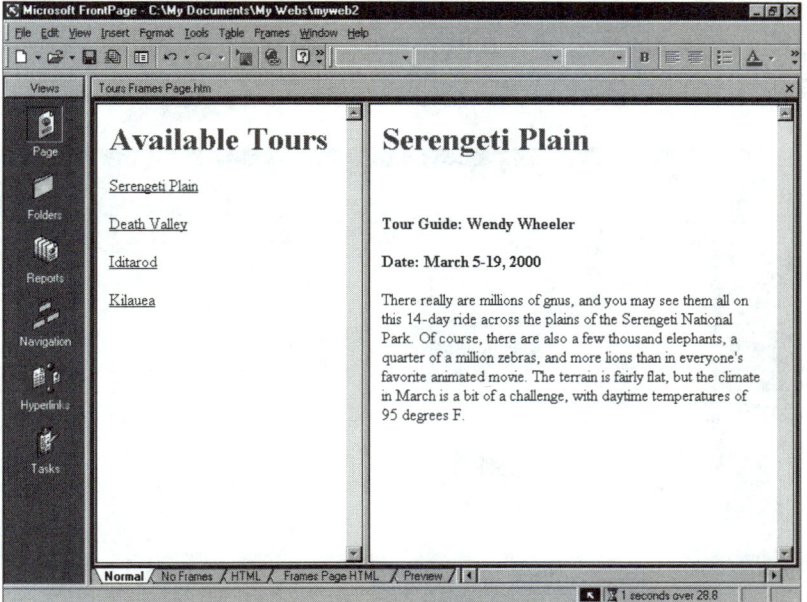

2. Save all your changes to all the pages and then close the web by choosing Close Web from the File menu. (You'll use the web you created in Part One for the remainder of the chapter.)

Closing a web

Creating Tables

Tables provide visual summaries of information and enable you to quickly grasp relationships that might be lost in narrative explanations. Tables can also be used to create more complex page layouts (see the tip on page 94).

Creating tables in FrontPage is a simple process. You specify the number of columns and rows and then leave it to FrontPage to figure out the initial settings, which you can always change later. To demonstrate how easy the process is, you'll add a table that displays tour costs to the Services page of the Exotic Excursions web. Follow these steps:

1. Choose Open Web from the File menu, navigate to the My Webs folder, select Myweb, and then click Open.

Opening a web

2. Now click the Open button on the toolbar and double-click services.htm.

The Insert Table button

3. Scroll to the bottom of the Our Destinations page, click an insertion point at the end of the *To the Brink and Back* paragraph and then press Enter twice.

4. Click the Insert Table button on the Standard toolbar to drop down a column/row grid, like this one:

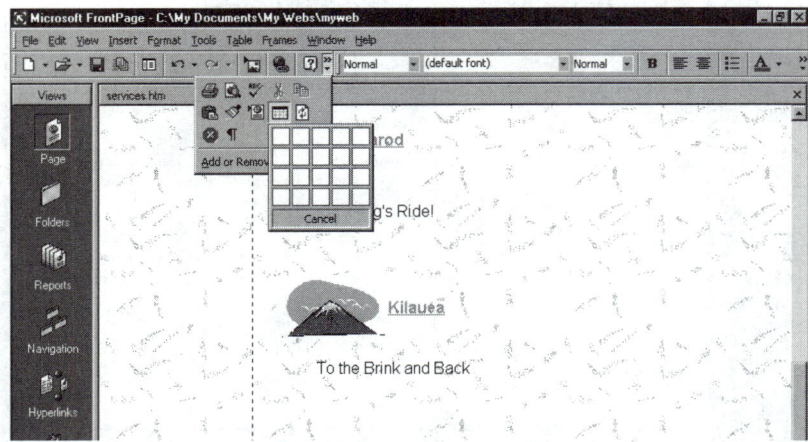

Other ways to create tables

You can create a table with specific column widths by choosing Insert and then Table from the Table menu and entering specifications in the Insert Table dialog box. Yet another way to create a table is to use the Draw Table button on the Tables toolbar. Click an insertion point where you want the table on the page and then click the button to activate the Draw Table tool. Drag the pencil-shaped pointer diagonally to draw a box. When the box is the size you want for the table, release the mouse button. Next draw horizontal and vertical lines to create rows and columns. To remove a line, click the Eraser button on the Tables toolbar to activate the Eraser tool and drag over the line you want to erase. You can erase one border of a cell to merge cells either vertically or horizontally. To turn off either the Draw Table or Eraser tool, simply click its button to toggle it off. You can then edit and format the table just as you would any other table.

5. Point to the top left square, hold down the left mouse button, and drag the pointer across four columns and down five rows. The grid expands as you drag beyond its bottom edge, and FrontPage shows the size of the selection below the grid. When you release the mouse button, FrontPage inserts a table structure in the page like the one shown here:

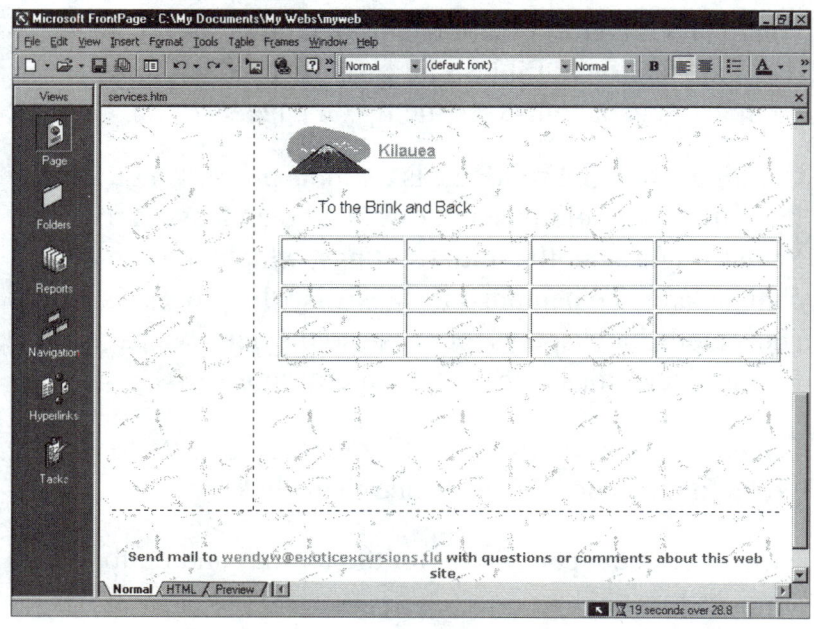

As you can see, FrontPage has created a table with four equal columns that span the width of the page's text column. (You can manually adjust the size of table rows and columns by moving the pointer over the row's bottom border or the column's right border and dragging in the appropriate direction.) The insertion point is in the first *cell* (the intersection of the first column and the first row). To enter information in this cell, all you have to do is type, like this:

Sizing columns and rows

1. Type *Tour Name* in the first cell and press Tab. The insertion point moves to the next cell on the right.

2. Type *Tour Price*, press Tab, type *Gear Costs*, press Tab, type *Travel Costs*, and press Tab. Here are the results so far:

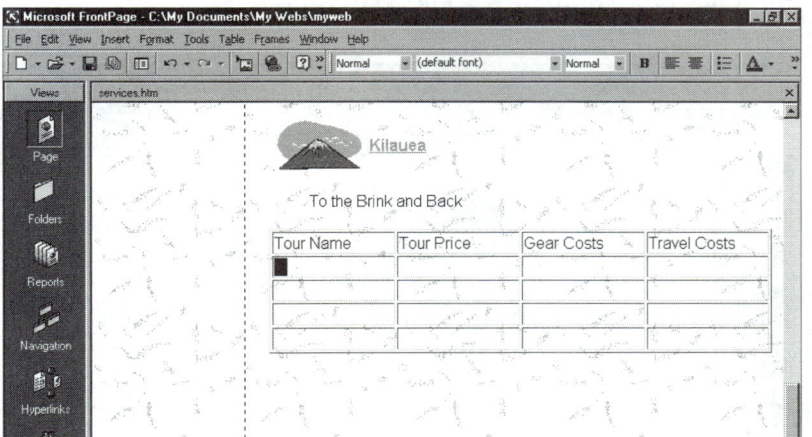

Notice that pressing Tab at the end of the first row moved the insertion point to the first cell in the second row.

3. Finish the table by typing the entries shown below, pressing Tab to move from cell to cell. (Pressing Shift+Tab moves the insertion point to the previous cell, and you can also use the Arrow keys and the mouse to move around.)

Serengeti Plain	*$1200*	*$200*	*$1000*
Death Valley	*$480*	*$100*	*$320*
Iditarod	*$650*	*$350*	*$440*
Kilauea	*$720*	*$150*	*$675*

Looking over the table, you can probably see one or two changes that would make it more effective. We discuss ways to edit tables in the next section.

Deleting/inserting rows and columns

To delete one or more rows or columns, select them and choose Delete Cells from the Table menu. (You can also click the Delete Cells button on the Tables toolbar.) To delete the entire table, select it and press Delete. To insert rows or columns, select the number of rows or columns you want to add and choose Insert and then Rows Or Columns from the Table menu. Select the options you want, including where you want the rows or columns inserted, and click OK. You can also use the Insert Rows or Insert Columns button on the Tables toolbar to insert the selected number of rows or columns with the default location setting displayed in the Insert Rows Or Columns dialog box.

Rearranging a Table

You can rearrange the rows and columns in a table in much the same way that you rearrange text. Let's switch the Travel Costs column with the Gear Costs column:

Selecting columns, rows, and the table

1. Click any cell in the Travel Costs column and choose Select and then Column from the Table menu. (You can choose Select and then Row to select the row containing the active cell, or Select and then Table to select the entire table.)

Moving columns

2. Point to the selected column, hold down the mouse button, drag the shadow insertion point to the beginning of the Gear Costs heading, and release the mouse button. As a result, the Travel Costs column moves to the left of the Gear Costs column, and the table now looks like this:

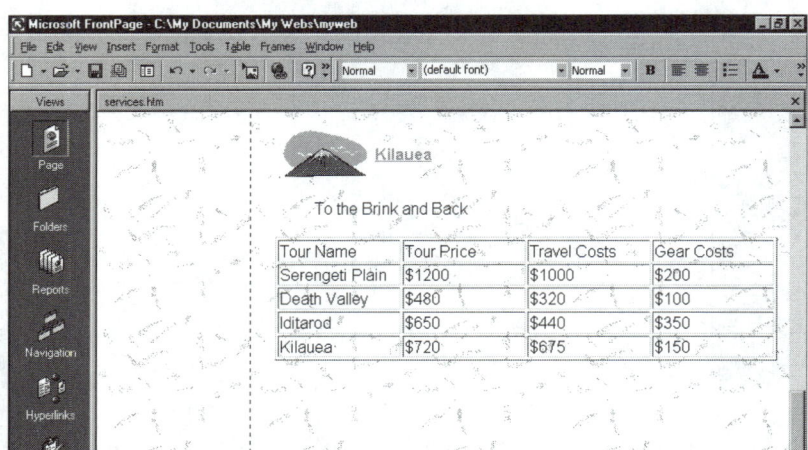

Setting table properties

To set a table's position on a page, right-click the table and choose Table Properties from the shortcut menu. Select the alignment you want. To modify the way text flows around the table, select an option from the Float drop-down list. (If you don't want text to flow around a table, select Default.) You can also specify the amount of space between the borders of a cell and its contents, enter how much space to allow between cells, and change the table's borders and background. (See the tip on the facing page for information about table borders.)

Adding a Title

Suppose you want to add a row above the table to contain a title. The first step is to insert a new row, which you can do easily with the aid of the Tables toolbar. Here are the steps:

1. Right-click any toolbar and choose Tables from the shortcut menu. Then double-click the toolbar's title bar to dock it below the Standard and Formatting toolbars.

2. Click an insertion point anywhere in the first row of the table and choose Select and then Row from the Table menu.

3. Click the Insert Rows button on the Tables toolbar. FrontPage inserts the number of rows you selected—in this case, one.

The Insert Rows button

Next you need to join the cells of the new row to create one large cell to accommodate the table's title. Joining cells is a simple procedure, as you'll see if you follow these steps:

1. Select the first row of the table and click the Merge Cells button on the Tables toolbar. FrontPage combines the cells into one large cell that spans the table.

The Merge Cells button

2. Now enter the table's title. Click an insertion point in the top row, type *Exotic Excursions Bicycle Tour Prices*, press Shift+Enter, and type *2000*.

Formatting a Table

Having made all the necessary structural changes to the table, let's add some finishing touches. First you'll format the title and headings, like this:

1. Select the first two rows of the table by dragging through them. Then click the Center button and press Home to remove the highlighting and view the results.

2. To make the table title and the headings in the *Tour Name* column bold, point above and to the left of the word *Exotic* in the title and when the pointer turns into a down arrow, click the mouse button once. (FrontPage considers the merged cell to be part of the table's first column.) Then click the Bold button.

3. Next select the headings for the second through fourth columns and make them bold.

4. Now select the dollar amounts and click the Align Right button on the Formatting toolbar.

Before we end this section, let's give the table a caption. When you add a caption to a table, the caption text remains attached to the table even though it does not appear in the table itself. If you move the table to another location, the caption moves as well. (See the tip on page 92 for information about moving tables.) Follow the steps on the next page.

Changing table borders

By default, FrontPage gives tables a border and gridlines. If you want a table to have no border or gridlines, right-click the table and choose Table Properties from the shortcut menu. In the Size box of the Borders section, enter 0 as the width of the border. FrontPage then delineates the table and its cells with dotted lines so that you can edit the table while working on the Normal tab. (The dotted lines disappear when you switch to the Preview tab to see how the table will look when you publish it.) If you aren't using a theme, you can also set border colors in the Table Properties dialog box. (If you are using a theme and you want to change the table border color, you must modify the theme as described in the tip on page 42.) To specify only one color, select a color from the Color drop-down list in the Borders section. To specify a two-color border, which gives your table a three-dimensional look, select colors from the Light Border and Dark Border drop-down lists.

Adding a table caption

1. With the insertion point located anywhere in the table, choose Insert and then Caption from the Table menu. FrontPage moves the insertion point directly above the table.

2. Type the following paragraph:

   The travel and gear costs shown in the table below are estimates. Your costs may vary depending on where you live.

Moving the caption

3. The caption doesn't look very good at the top of the table, so right-click it and choose Caption Properties from the shortcut menu to display this dialog box:

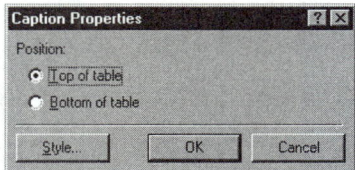

4. Select the Bottom Of Table option and click OK.

5. Change the word *below* to *above* and rebreak the caption at the end of the first sentence. Then make the entire caption italic. Here are the results:

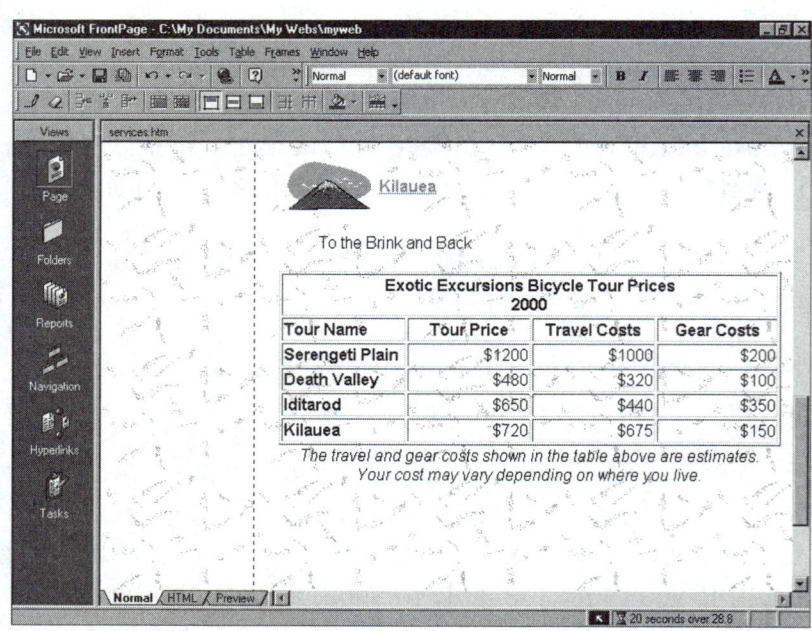

6. Turn off the Tables toolbar and then save your work.

> **Using tables for page layout**
>
> When laying out the content of your pages, you might want to experiment with using tables. Besides giving you a way to display information in the traditional columnar format, tables can be used to arrange all types of content on your pages in a variety of ways. For example, you might insert a graphic image in one cell and then describe the graphic in the adjacent cell. You can change the background shading and borders for individual cells to create a more visually appealing layout. You can also use tables to create a page with multiple columns of text. Be sure to check out the available templates on the General tab of the New dialog box first, though, to see whether the page layout you want to create already exists.

Creating Visitor Input Forms

In order for visitors to your Web site to request more information about a product or service or order an item via the site, they must be able to fill in an input form. You might also want to use forms to gather marketing information about your products and services or feedback about your Web site. If you'll publish your web on a server than supports FrontPage Server Extensions, creating and using forms is a snap because a form handler takes care of processing the information you gather into a usable format.

A form consists of text entries that don't change, which are called *labels*, and associated areas that record each visitor's information, which are called *fields*. You set up the form using different types of fields for different types of information. Visitors complete the fields by typing in edit boxes or clicking options. They move from one field to the next by pressing the Tab key, skipping over the labels that describe the fields.

◀ **Labels and fields**

With FrontPage, you can easily add input forms to your pages either by using a predefined form or by creating one from scratch (see the tip on the next page).

Customizing a Placeholder Form

As you may recall, you added a Suggestions form page to the Exotic Excursions web on page 44. In this section, you will edit the placeholder form on this page to meet your needs. After you finish creating the form, we'll discuss how to collect the information your visitors enter in it. Follow these steps to get started:

1. Open the Suggestions page of the Exotic Excursions web and scroll to the placeholder form.

2. Select the paragraph that begins *What kind of comment* and replace it with *Please enter the location of the bicycle tour you want to suggest*.

3. Type a colon (:) and a space and then choose Form and One-Line Text Box from the Insert menu to insert a text-box field.

◀ **Inserting form fields**

4. Select the options below the new field and press Delete.

5. Next select the line that begins *What about us* and replace it with *Please enter the estimated number of days needed for this tour*.

6. Repeat step 3 to insert another one-line text box.

7. Delete the next line of placeholder form fields. Then replace the word *comments* in the next paragraph with *description of the tour*. Here are the results so far:

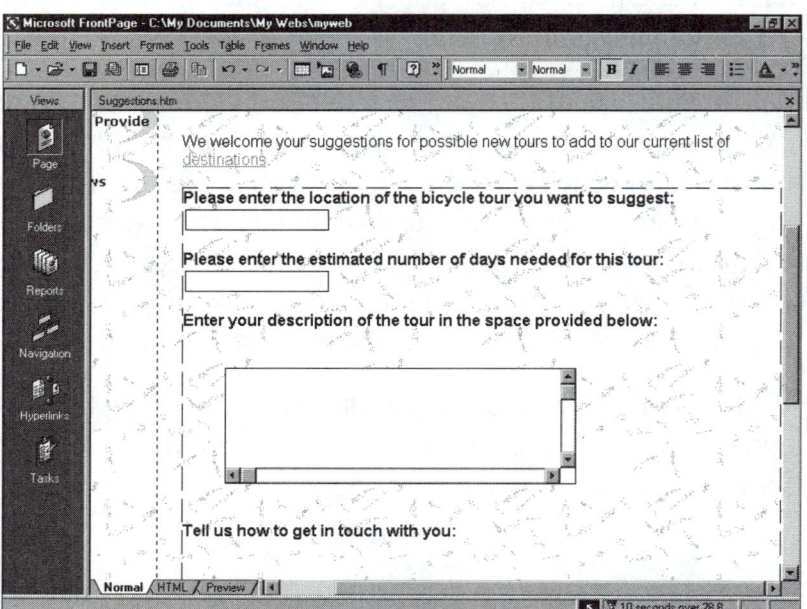

Creating a form from scratch

To add a form to a page, choose Form and then Form from the Insert menu. FrontPage inserts a form area surrounded by a dotted rectangular frame, as well as Submit and Reset buttons. You can then enter text and add form fields as described in the adjacent section. If you want to create a new form page with the help of a wizard, choose New and then Page from the File menu, select the Form Page Wizard icon on the General tab, and click OK. The wizard then walks you through the steps for creating the form.

The field below the *Enter your description* paragraph is called a *scrolling text box*. It allows the visitor to enter multiple lines of text rather than just one.

Now let's finish up the form by adding some other types of fields. You'll start with a set of *radio buttons*, which work in forms the same way they do in dialog boxes. Just as you can select only one radio station at a time on a car radio, visitors can select only one radio-button option at a time. You should use radio buttons when you want to require the visitor to make a selection from a predefined list. You set them up like this:

1. Select the paragraph that begins *Tell us* and replace it with *Can we e-mail you if we would like more information?*

2. Type a space, followed by *Yes* and another space. Then choose Form and then Radio Button from the Insert menu.   ◀── **Inserting radio buttons**

3. Type a space, followed by *No* and another space. Then insert another radio button. Notice that FrontPage designates only one radio button as selected.

4. Press Enter and then type *If "yes," please enter your name and e-mail address.*

5. In the table below, point to the left of Tel and when the pointer changes to a black, right-pointing arrow, click to select the row. Then right-click the selection and choose Delete Cells from the shortcut menu.

6. Repeat step 5 to delete the Fax row.

   For marketing purposes, you want to know how visitors learned about Exotic Excursions, but you want the responses to be structured so that you can tabulate the data. If you use a regular text box, you will have too many variables to deal with. To collect this type of information, you could use radio buttons, but to conserve space you can instead use a *drop-down menu* of options like the ones you see on toolbars and in dialog boxes, from which visitors can make a selection. Follow these steps:

1. Point to the left of the check box and the *Please contact me* paragraph and click to select the entire line. Then press Enter to both delete the existing text and start a new line.

2. Type *How did you hear about Exotic Excursions?* and press the spacebar. Then select any word in the paragraph above, click the Format Painter button on the Standard toolbar, and select the new paragraph to make its formatting consistent with the rest of the form.

3. Press End to move to the end of the paragraph, and choose Form and then Drop-Down Menu from the Insert menu. Front-Page inserts a drop-down menu, as shown on the next page.   ◀── **Inserting a drop-down menu**

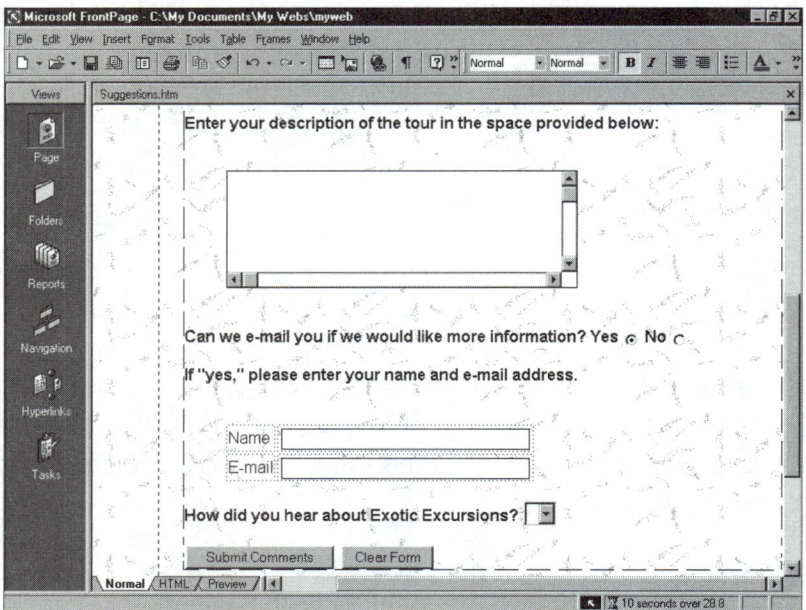

The drop-down menu doesn't do you much good if it doesn't contain options. In the next section, you'll remedy that situation as you learn how to change the properties of form fields.

Modifying Field Properties

After you add a field to a form, you can easily modify its properties to suit your needs. As we just mentioned, you need to modify the properties of the drop-down menu to include the options you want your visitors to select from. You also want to specify properties for some of the one-line text boxes you added. Follow these steps:

1. Right-click the drop-down menu field and choose Form Field Properties from the shortcut menu to display this dialog box:

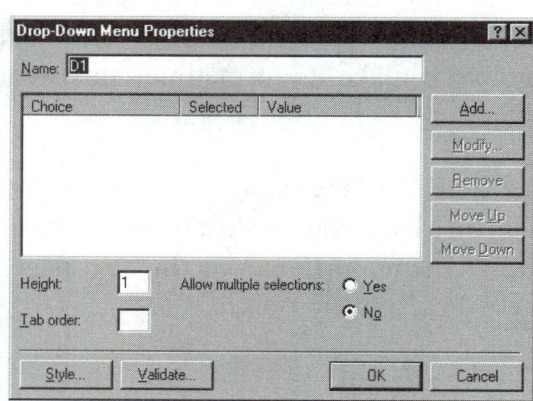

More drop-down menu options

In the Drop-Down Menu Properties dialog box, you can modify, delete, and change the order of the menu choices by clicking their respective buttons. You can also change the height of the menu so that it displays more than one option by entering a number in the Height box. To allow visitors to select more than one menu option, click Yes as the Allow Multiple Selections setting. (To allow multiple selections, check box form fields are usually a better format to use.)

2. Type *Referred_by* in the Name edit box. When you collect the data entered by your visitors, the FrontPage form handler will now associate the value selected from the drop-down menu with the name *Referred_by*. (This name does not appear on the actual form on the page.)

   ◄ **Specifying field names**

3. To add options to the menu, click the Add button to display this dialog box:

   ◄ **Entering drop-down menu options**

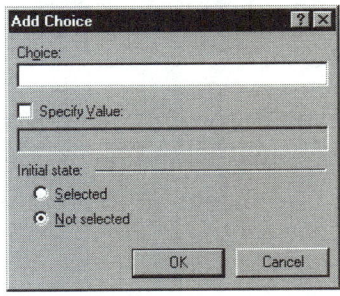

4. Type *Friend* in the Choice box. In the Initial State section, click the Selected option so that the word *Friend* is selected by default. Then click OK.

5. Repeat steps 3 and 4 to add the options listed below to the drop-down menu. (For these entries, leave the Not Selected option selected in the Initial State section.)

   Word of mouth
   Bicycle club
   Bicycle shop
   Web search
   Promotional mailing
   Other

6. After completing the entries, click OK to close the Drop-Down Menu Properties dialog box.

   Now let's set some properties for the two one-line text boxes:

1. Scroll to the beginning of the form and double-click the first one-line text box to display the Text Box Properties dialog box, which is shown on the next page.

> **Requiring an entry**
>
> When setting properties for text boxes, radio buttons, or drop-down menus, you can click the Validate button to set data entry rules for the selected form field. Validation options vary for each form field type. However, you can click the Data Required check box in any Validation dialog box to require that visitors select an option in the specified field.

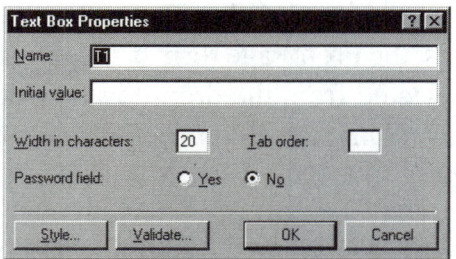

Changing a field's width

2. Type *Location* as the name. Then change the Width In Characters setting to *50* and click OK. FrontPage resizes the text box to accommodate the new setting.

The Increase Indent button

3. Now to make this text box more like the scrolling text box, click an insertion point at the end of the paragraph above, press Enter, and then click the Increase Indent button on the Formatting toolbar.

Adding validation rules

4. Next double-click the second one-line text box, enter *Days* as the name, *2* as the width, and then click Validate to display these options shown on the facing page.

Customizing buttons

By default, FrontPage creates Submit and Reset buttons at the bottom of every input form. You can easily change the name of a button. Right-click it and choose Form Field Properties from the shortcut menu. Then change the entry in the Value/Label box. (FrontPage adjusts the size of the button to fit its new name.) To change the action the button performs when it is clicked, select the appropriate option in the Button Type section. Then click OK. To create a new button, choose Form and then Push Button from the Insert menu. After FrontPage creates the button, right-click it and change its properties in the usual way.

Setting the tab order of fields

When visitors want to move around an input form in a Web page, they can simply press the Tab key to move from field to field. By default, pressing the Tab key activates the fields in order from top to bottom on the page. If you want to specify a different tab order, double-click a field to display its properties and enter a number in the Tab Order box. Repeat this step for all other fields you want to customize. (Custom tab orders work only with Internet Explorer 4.0 or later. Other browsers use the default tab order.)

Confirmation pages

After visitors type information in an input form and click the Submit button, they see a confirmation page that shows them the information they just entered and confirms that the data has been sent. You can use the default confirmation page created by FrontPage for input forms, or you can create one of your own. To designate a page you have created as the confirmation page, display the Form Properties dialog box and then click the Options button. Click the Confirmation Page tab, type the URL of the confirmation page you want to use, and click OK twice.

Chapter 4 Creating a More Complex Web

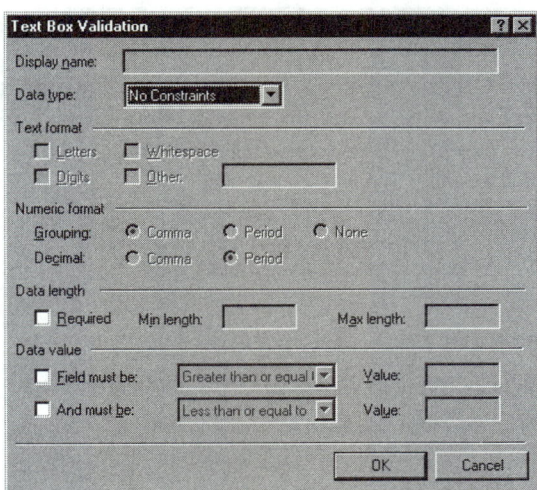

Here, you can enter validation rules that the entered data must comply with. If the data does not comply with these rules, the Web browser will display an error message, and visitors must reenter the data following the specified guidelines.

5. Click the arrow to the right of the Data Type edit box and select Integer so that visitors can enter only numeric values in this field.

6. Click None as the Grouping option in the Numeric Format section so that only whole numbers can be entered, and not numbers like 7.5.

7. Click OK twice. Then save the page.

Previewing an Input Form

After you have added all the form fields you want and have modified their properties as necessary, you will want to preview the form on the Preview tab. There you can check the form's layout, as well as experiment with filling in its fields. To preview and test the Suggestions form, follow these steps:

1. With the Suggestions page displayed in page view, click the Preview tab to display your form as shown on the next page. (We've turned off the toolbars so that you can see all the fields.)

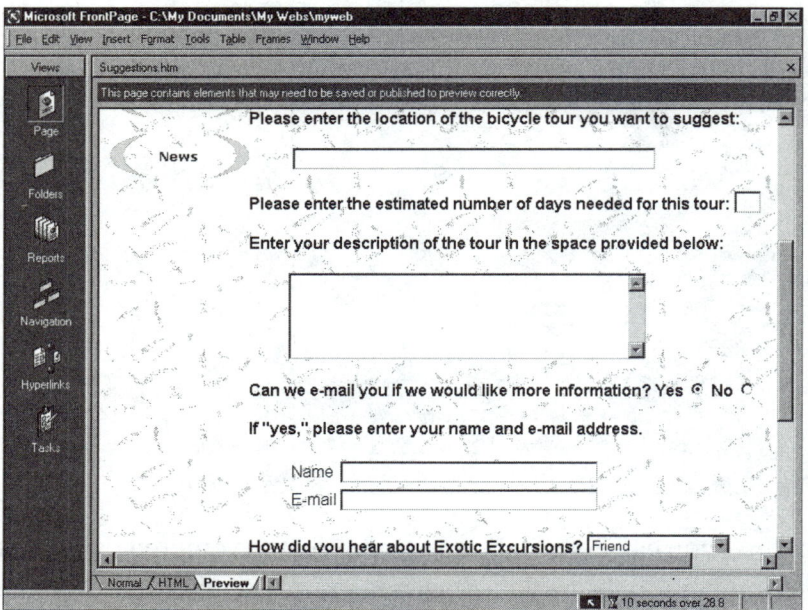

2. Click an insertion point in the first text box and type *Siberia*.

Moving around a form

3. Press Tab. The insertion point jumps over the text paragraph to the next text-box field.

4. Type *20* and press Tab. Again, the insertion point skips over the text paragraph to the scrolling text box field.

5. Type a short description for a bicycle trip in Siberia.

6. With the Yes radio-button option selected, type your name in the Name edit box, press Tab, type your e-mail address in the E-Mail edit box, and press Tab again.

Adding search capabilities

If your Web server supports the Microsoft FrontPage Server Extensions (see page 69), FrontPage automatically creates a text index of the words used in your web. You can then add a search form so that visitors can search your web for specific words or phrases. To add a search form to a page, click an insertion point where you want the search form to appear and choose Component and then Search Form from the Insert menu. In the Search Form Properties dialog box, make any necessary changes and then click OK. Remember that searches conducted through the form are only as accurate as the index. As you add text to your web, FrontPage updates the index. However, if you delete text, FrontPage doesn't remove those words from the index. To update the index after you delete text, you need to recalculate the hyperlinks in your web. To do this, choose recalculate hyperlinks from the Tools menu and then in the Recalculate Hyperlinks dialog box, simply click Yes to begin the process, which may take several minutes.

Chapter 4 Creating a More Complex Web

7. Click the arrow to the right of the drop-down menu field and select Web Search from the list. The form now looks as shown here:

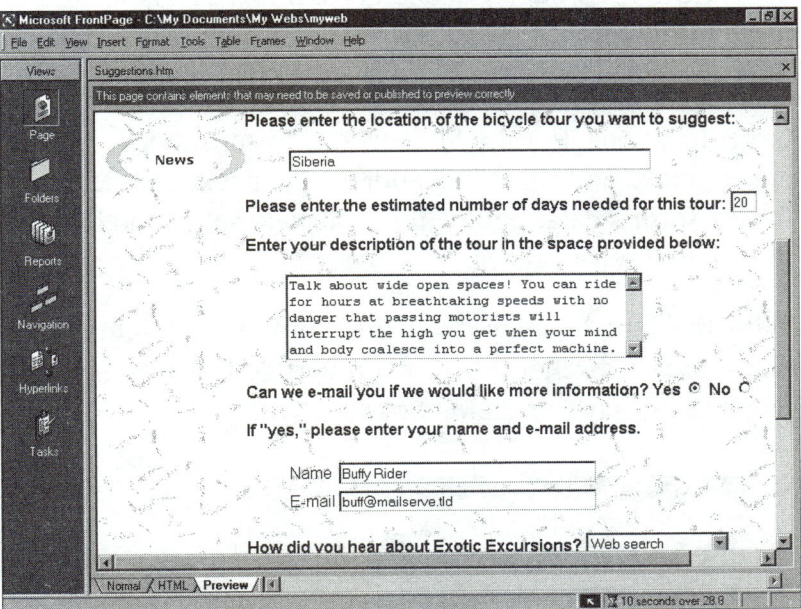

8. Click the Clear Form button at the bottom of the form to remove your test entries and then click the Normal tab.

Collecting Data from an Input Form

After you create an input form, you will want to define a target location for the information submitted by visitors to your Web site. The type of target you use will depend on what you plan to do with your data. You have these three data collection options:

- **An e-mail address.** Data will be sent in an e-mail message to the specified address as soon as visitors click the Submit Comments button. Although this option gives you the data immediately, it does not send it in a format that can be easily converted for use in a database or other type of document.

◄ Data collection options

- **A text file.** The data will be more difficult to open but will be organized so that each field is separated by a comma, tab, or space, making it easy to import into a database or spreadsheet.

- **A database.** The data will be sent directly to the database you specify, provided the database has been set up as a system data source name and a connection has been established to the database in FrontPage. (Consult FrontPage's Help feature for more information.)

Multiple targets ➤ To make your decision easier, you can use a combination of target locations. For the Suggestions form, suppose you decide to make both an e-mail address and a text file the targets for the form's data. Follow these steps to set up the form for this type of retrieval:

1. With the form displayed on the Normal tab, right-click a blank area and choose Form Properties from the shortcut menu to display this dialog box:

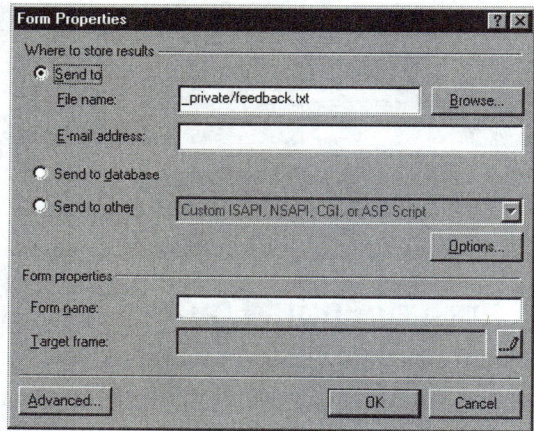

2. Check that the Send To option is selected and then type *info@exoticexcursions.tld* in the E-mail Address edit box.

3. If you wanted the data to be sent only to the e-mail address, you would delete the entry in the File Name box. However, because you want to collect the information in a text file as well, leave the filename as is.

4. Next click the Options button and click the E-mail Results tab to display the options shown at the top of the facing page.

Chapter 4 Creating a More Complex Web

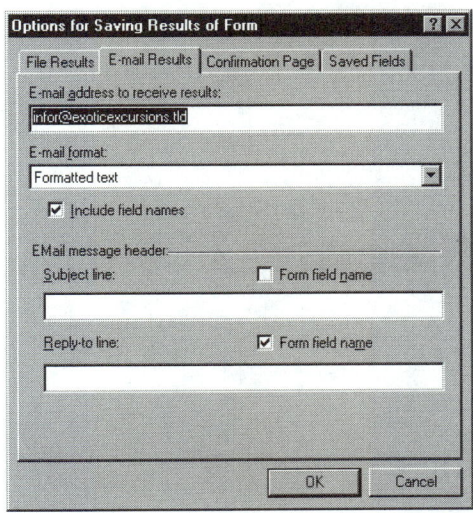

To change the way the data is formatted in the message, you can select an option from the E-mail Format drop-down list. You can also specify whether or not to include the field names as well as the field values in the e-mail message.

5. Type *Tour Suggestions* in the Subject Line box so that you will recognize any e-mail messages with this heading as containing data generated by the form. Click OK twice to implement the changes.

    Specifying the message subject

6. If FrontPage displays a message box saying that either you are using a disk-based server (your own computer) or your server's FrontPage Server Extensions have not yet been configured to send e-mail, click OK and then click Cancel to close the Options dialog box. You can then set up data collection when you know that the server can handle the form properly.

That ends our discussion of forms. As you continue to experiment with the techniques described in this chapter, you will probably find other ways to use the features to improve your webs. In the next chapter, we'll show you some of the more complex graphical and interactive elements you can add to your pages.

Adding Special Effects

In this chapter, you learn how to add various special effects to your pages. You look at more advanced graphics techniques, including hotspots. You then add hover buttons, marquees, and hit counters. You also see how to insert sound, video, and non–HTML components.

The special effects you add to the sample web not only add interest to a page but can be useful ways of presenting information. These effects can be incorporated into any type of Web page.

Web pages created and concepts covered:

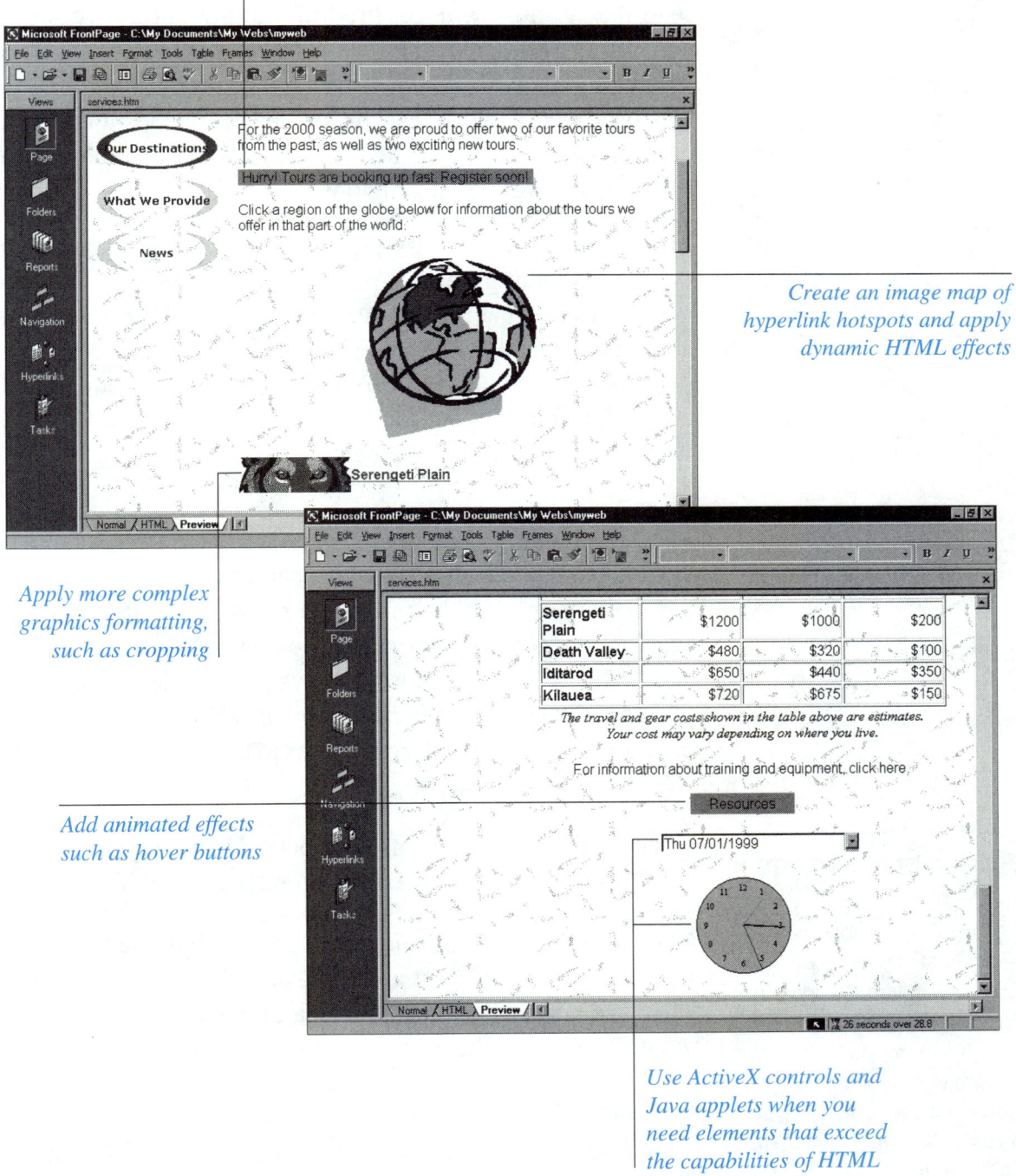

Draw attention to information with a scrolling marquee

Create an image map of hyperlink hotspots and apply dynamic HTML effects

Apply more complex graphics formatting, such as cropping

Add animated effects such as hover buttons

Use ActiveX controls and Java applets when you need elements that exceed the capabilities of HTML

Special effects are used extensively in many Web sites. They are most often designed to draw attention and to display information in a way that is not possible with regular formatting. If special effects are overused, they can detract from a Web site's message or take so long to download that visitors will get tired of waiting and move on to something else. But if they are reserved for those occasions when they can really enhance a page's looks or functionality, special effects can increase the amount of time visitors spend at your site and as a result, increase its effectiveness as a means of conveying information.

In this chapter, we start by expanding on what you learned in Chapter 2 about graphics. We show you additional ways to apply formatting and how to create hotspots. Next you learn about elements that change or are updated when visitors display the page or point to certain items. You also add sound and video files to your pages. Finally, you look at ways to work with non–HTML elements.

More About Graphics

In Chapter 2, you learned how to insert graphics from the Clip Art Gallery and how to move and resize them. FrontPage's graphics capabilities far exceed these simple manipulations, and in this section, you look at ways to enhance the graphics you use in your webs to create more visual interest. As a demonstration, you'll add more graphics to the Exotic Excursions web. Follow these steps:

1. Open the Exotic Excursions web located in the Myweb folder and then display the Our Destinations page (services.htm).

2. Click the graphic of the lion's head to the left of the Serengeti Plain heading to select it and to display the Pictures toolbar. Then use ScreenTips to get an idea of what you can do with the graphic using the buttons on this toolbar.

Formatting a Graphic

After inserting a graphic in a page, you can accomplish most formatting tasks with the aid of the Pictures toolbar. Suppose you want to change the graphic of the lion's head so that only

> **Adjusting brightness and contrast**
>
> You can adjust the brightness or contrast of the graphics you add to a page. To adjust the brightness, select the graphic and click either the More Brightness or Less Brightness button on the Pictures toolbar. To adjust the contrast, select the graphic and click either the More Contrast or Less Contrast button.

Chapter 5 Adding Special Effects

its eyes are displayed. To achieve this effect, you need to change the size of the frame without changing the size of the graphic itself, thereby "cropping" away the parts you don't want to be visible. You cannot crop a graphic for which you have specified a size, so you first need to return the graphic to its original size. Follow these steps:

Cropping graphics

1. Right-click the selected graphic and choose Picture Properties from the shortcut menu. Then click the Appearance tab to display the options shown earlier on page 37.

2. Click the Specify Size check box to toggle it off and click OK. FrontPage enlarges the graphic to its original size.

Now let's crop the lion graphic:

1. With the graphic selected, click the Crop button on the Pictures toolbar to turn on the cropping tool. A dashed border with white *crop handles* surrounds the graphic.

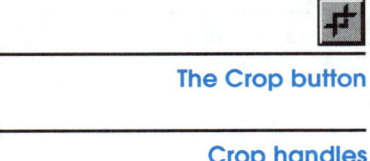

The Crop button

Crop handles

2. Point to the crop handle in the middle of the bottom border. Then drag upward until the border is just below the lion's eyes.

3. Next point to the crop handle in the middle of the top border and drag downward to crop away the lion's ears.

4. Click the Crop button again to toggle off the cropping tool and to crop away the parts of the graphic you don't want. Here are the results:

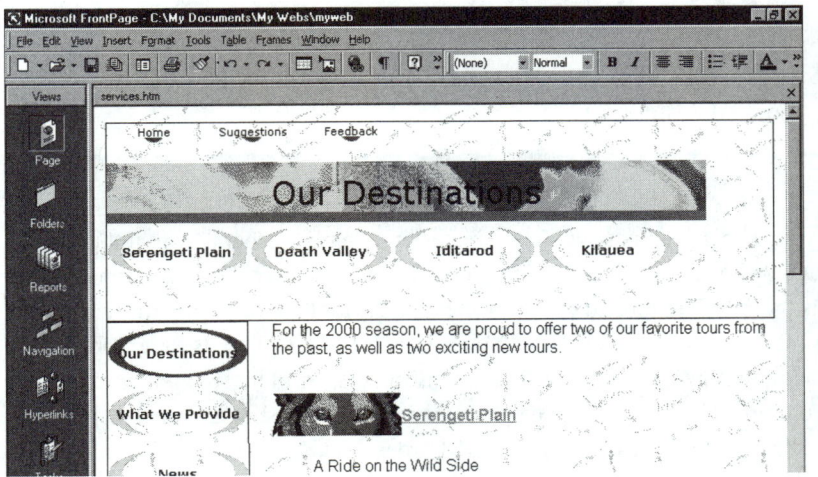

Rotating and flipping graphics

After inserting a graphic on a page, you can rotate or flip it. First select it and then click the Rotate Left button on the Pictures toolbar to rotate the graphic 90 degrees counterclockwise or the Rotate Right button to rotate it 90 degrees clockwise. If you click the Flip Vertical button, FrontPage turns the graphic upside down. To create a mirror image, click the Flip Horizontal button.

The Restore button

If you decide you don't like the way you've cropped the graphic (or any other formatting effect applied to a graphic), you can click the Restore button on the Pictures toolbar to return the graphic to its original settings.

To give a graphic more definition, you can surround it with a border. In this case, suppose you want to use a border that has a beveled effect so that the graphic will look like a button. Follow these steps:

1. Select the graphic of the lion's eyes and then display the Appearance tab of the Picture Properties dialog box.

2. Change the Border Thickness setting to 2 and click OK.

The Bevel button

3. Next click the Bevel button on the Pictures toolbar to give the graphic a three-dimensional appearance, as shown here:

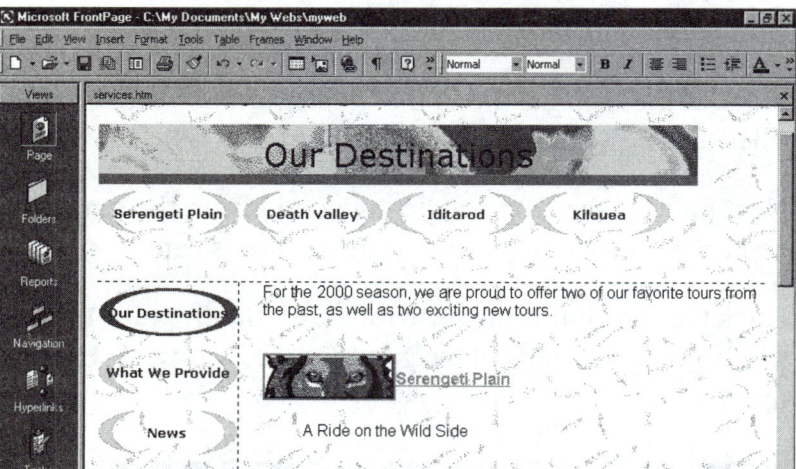

4. Click the Save button to save the graphic in its current state as part of your web.

Creating thumbnails

To decrease the download time of your site's graphics, you can create thumbnails of them. A thumbnail is a scaled-down version of a graphic that a visitor can click to view the full-size version. To convert a graphic into a thumbnail, select the graphic and click the Auto Thumbnail button on the Pictures toolbar. FrontPage instantly creates the thumbnail as well as a hyperlink to the full-size version. (You cannot create thumbnails for graphics that are already smaller than the default thumbnail size, that contain a hyperlink or hotspot, or that include animation.) To change the default properties for thumbnails, choose Page Options from the Tools menu and then display the AutoThumbnail tab. Here, you can adjust options for the default size, border thickness, and whether or not the thumbnail has a beveled edge.

5. Preview the Our Destinations page and check that the lion graphic's hyperlink to the Serengeti Plain page is still intact.

Using Hotspots

When you create a graphic hyperlink, clicking anywhere on the graphic moves your visitors to the hyperlink's target. Under certain circumstances, you might want to use only part of a graphic as a hyperlink. The hyperlinked part is called a *hotspot*. Although hotspots are invisible, visitors know when they are pointing to one because the pointer changes to a white pointing hand, and clicking the hotspot displays the designated target as usual. In addition to creating hotspots on graphics, you can add them to animated GIF-format graphics and videos. ← **Recognizing hotspots**

A graphic that contains more than one hotspot is called an *image map*. Image maps are particularly useful as a sort of topic table of contents. For example, in the Exotic Excursions web, a page devoted to a discussion of the equipment suitable for a specific tour might display a graphic of a bicycle with different components designated as hotspots. When visitors click a specific component, such as the back wheel, their Web browser might jump to a page listing the component's minimum and ideal specifications for that particular tour. ← **Image maps**

As an example of how to use hotspots, let's insert a globe graphic on the Our Destinations page and add hotspots that link visitors to the individual tour pages. Follow these steps:

1. On the Our Destinations page, click an insertion point at the end of the first paragraph and press Enter to start a new paragraph.

2. Type the following sentence and then press Enter twice:

   Click a region of the globe below for information about the tours we offer in that part of the world.

3. Press the Up Arrow key to leave some space between the graphic you'll insert and the lion graphic below. Next choose Picture and then Clip Art from the Insert menu to display the Clip Art Gallery window.

4. Display the contents of the Maps category and insert the third globe graphic.

5. Resize the graphic so that it is about two-thirds its original size. Then center the graphic on the page, as shown here:

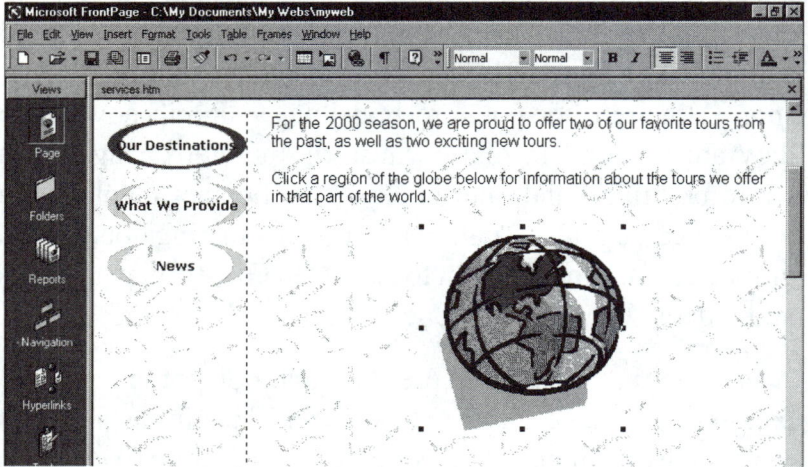

Now you're ready to add the hotspots to the graphic. With FrontPage, you can draw a circle, rectangle, or polygon on a graphic to designate the hotspot. Which you use depends on the graphic. Here's how to use circles:

The Circular Hotspot button

1. With the graphic selected, click the Circular Hotspot button on the Pictures toolbar.

2. Point to Africa, which is only partially displayed on the right side of the graphic, and drag to create a small circle. When you release the mouse button, FrontPage displays the Create Hyperlink dialog box shown earlier on page 44.

Adding text hotspots

You can add text hotspots to graphics that jump to their target locations when clicked just like regular hotspots. Select the graphic and then click the Text button on the Pictures toolbar. When FrontPage displays a text box with an insertion point, type the text you want. If necessary, resize or move the text box as you would any other object. To change the font color, simply select the text and use the Font Color button on the Formatting toolbar. To define the hyperlink, double-click a border of the text box and create the hyperlink as usual.

Chapter 5 Adding Special Effects   113

3. Select serv01.htm (the Serengeti Plain page) and click OK to create a hyperlink to that tour's page.

4. Next click the Circular Hotspot button and draw a circle over Southern California. Designate serv02.htm (the Death Valley page) as the hyperlink's target.

5. Repeat this procedure to create circular hotspots over Alaska for the Iditarod tour and Hawaii for the Kilauea tours. (Hawaii does not appear on the map, so you will need to create the hotspot in its approximate location in the Pacific Ocean.)

6. Click anywhere outside the graphic and then reselect it to display the results shown here:

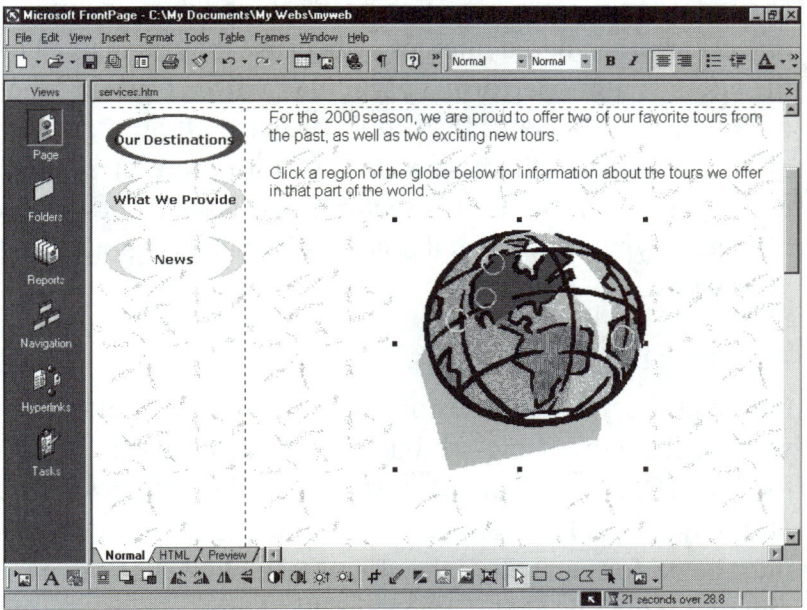

7. Save your work.

To test the image map you just created, follow these steps:

1. Click the Preview tab and move the pointer around the globe graphic.   ←   **Testing hotspots**

2. When the pointer changes to a pointing hand to indicate that you are over a hotspot, click once to move to the target you assigned to that hyperlink.

3. To return to the Our Destinations page, click its button on the navigation bar to the left. Then continue checking the hotspots until you have jumped to all four targets.

4. When you finish, click the Normal tab.

Editing hotspots

If you need to edit a hotspot, simply double-click it to redisplay the Create Hyperlink dialog box and make adjustments. To move, resize, or delete a hotspot, you use the same techniques you would for an entire graphic.

Working with Animated Objects

With FrontPage, you can add several types of animated objects to your pages. Animated objects move or in some way change when viewed in a Web browser, and some animated objects are considered interactive because they change when the site's visitors perform a particular action. Certain types of animation are useful for simply drawing attention to part of a page, while others provide a way to more effectively display information. In this section, you'll take a brief look at several types of animated objects you can incorporate into your webs.

Adding DHTML Effects

One method you can use for applying animated effects to your pages is by using the buttons on the DHTML Effects toolbar. (DHTML stands for *Dynamic HyperText Markup Language*.) DHTML effects are interactive because actions must be performed before the effects take place. Let's experiment with the DHTML Effects toolbar now.

Dynamic HyperText Markup Language

Suppose you decide that when visitors move to the Our Destinations page, the globe graphic that you inserted in the previous section should appear on the page with a spiral motion. Follow these steps to create this effect:

1. Right-click any toolbar and choose DHTML Effects from the shortcut menu.

2. If necessary, click the globe graphic to select it.

> **Other DHTML effects**
>
> You can apply several types of DHTML effects to text, graphics, and buttons on a web page. You define an event, such as pointing to the object with the mouse, and then specify the action, such as changing the color or style of text or switching one graphic for another. Remember, however, that too many effects can be irritating and can slow down your pages.

Chapter 5 Adding Special Effects

3. Click the arrow to the right of the On box on the DHTML Effects toolbar and select the Page Load option. ← **Specifying when to apply an effect**

4. Next click the arrow to the right of the Apply box and select Spiral. FrontPage surrounds the graphic with a border and light blue shading to indicate that you have applied a dynamic effect to it. ← **Selecting an effect**

5. Point to the graphic. ScreenTips briefly describes the effect you have specified, like this:

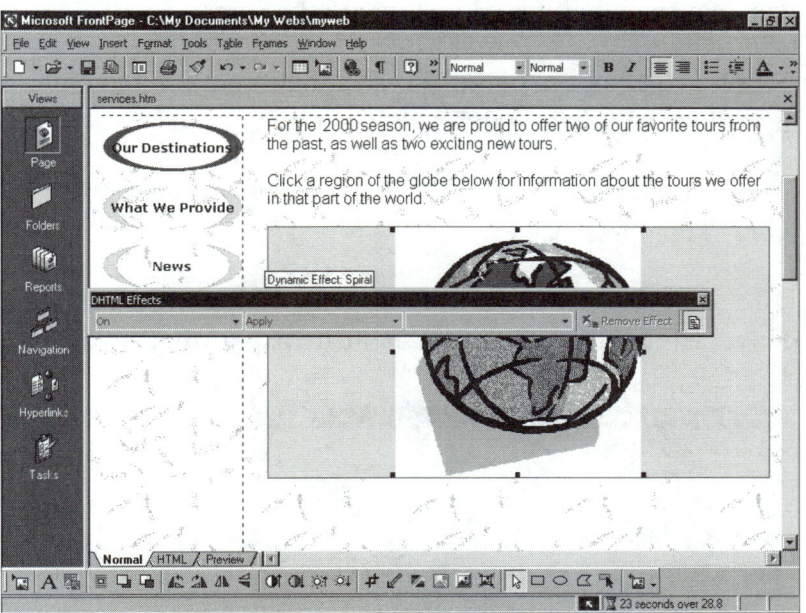

6. To test the effect, click the Preview tab. First FrontPage displays the page, and then the globe graphic spirals into view. Not a bad way to draw a visitor's attention!

7. Return to the Normal tab and turn off the DHTML Effects toolbar.

    If you want to remove a DHTML effect, you click the light blue area on one side of the graphic and then either click the Remove Effect button on the DHTML Effects toolbar or press Ctrl+Spacebar. You can then experiment with other effects. Bear in mind, though, that some Web browsers will substitute a different but similar effect if they can't produce the one you specified, or they may cause errors when the page is viewed.

The Remove Effect button

Creating a Hover Button

Like other buttons, *hover buttons* are hyperlinks. In addition, they display some type of special effect when visitors point to or click them. The special effect is caused by a program that is associated with the button, but you don't have to know anything about programming to create hover buttons. The program is included with FrontPage, allowing you to easily add this animated effect to your page.

Let's add a hover button to the Exotic Excursions web so that you can see what they do. Here are the steps:

1. Scroll to the bottom of the Our Destinations page and click an insertion point below the table's caption.

2. Type *For information about training and equipment, click here*. Then press Enter.

3. To insert the hover button, choose Component and then Hover Button from the Insert menu to display this dialog box:

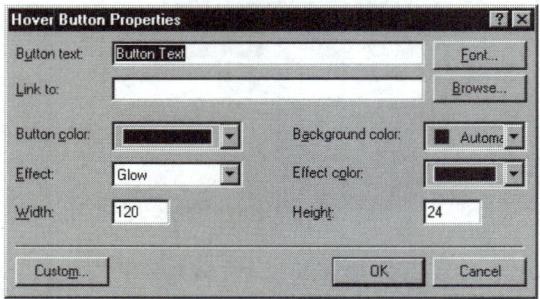

Naming the button → 4. In the Button Text box, type *Resources*.

Using graphics or sound in hover buttons

As well as using the effects available in the Hover Button Properties dialog box, you can add graphic or sound effects. To assign a graphic to a hover button, display the Hover Button Properties dialog box and click the Custom button. You can then specify that the graphic be used as the button's background or that the graphic be displayed when visitors point to the button. In the Custom section, enter the filename of the graphic you want to use in the Button edit box (for a background graphic) or in the On Hover edit box. (You can click the Browse button to navigate to the file.) Click OK. For the graphic to be displayed correctly, the size of the button must match the size of the graphic, so enter the dimensions of the graphic in the Width and Height boxes and click OK again. To assign a sound to a hover button, follow the same procedure except enter the sound's filename in the appropriate edit box in the Play Sound section of the Custom dialog box.

Chapter 5 Adding Special Effects 117

5. Click an insertion point in the Link To box and click the Browse button. Then double-click the Resources page in the list of files.

6. Click the arrow to the right of the Button Color edit box and select the second theme color (green).   ← **Specifying an effect**

7. Next click the arrow to the right of the Effect edit box and select Color Fill.

8. Finally, click the arrow to the right of the Effect Color edit box, click More Colors, select Orange, and click OK. Now when visitors point to the hover button, the color will change from green to orange.

9. Click OK to see these results:

The text doesn't stand out very well with its current formatting, so follow these steps to make some changes to the font size and color:

1. Right-click the button and choose Hover Button Properties from the shortcut menu. Then click the Font button to display a modified version of the Font dialog box. Change the font style to Bold, the size to 16, and the color to black. Click OK twice to close the Font dialog box and the Hover Button Properties dialog box.   ← **Formatting a button**

2. Click the Center button so that the button looks like this:

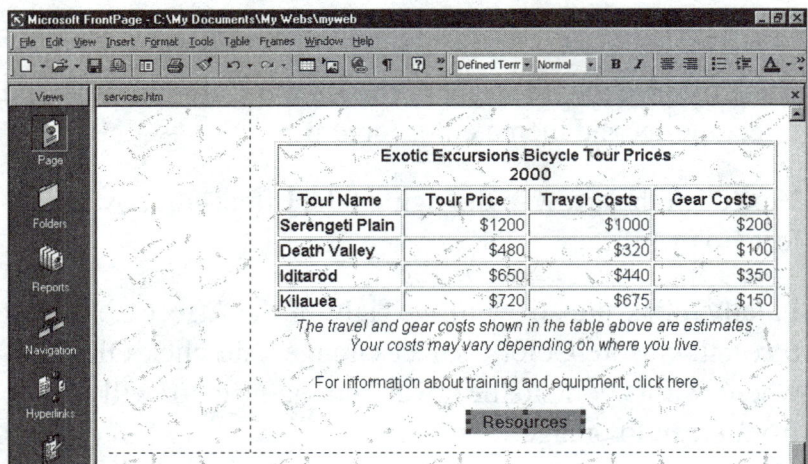

3. Now save the page to safeguard your changes.

As usual, test your work before moving on:

Testing a hover button

1. Click the Preview tab, watch the globe spiral into view, and scroll down the page.

2. Point to the hover button and check that the button changes colors as you specified.

3. Click the button to make sure that it moves to the correct page. Then return to the Our Destinations page.

If you want, experiment with other hover-button animation effects before you move on to the next section. (We discuss how to embed other programmed components on page 126.)

Creating a Marquee

You have undoubtedly seen web pages with moving text in a box. These elements are called *marquees*, and they are often used on commercial sites for displaying advertisements. (See the tip on page 120 for information about banner ads.) Because the text moves, it catches the eye and draws attention to its message. You may not want to display advertisements for outside products and services on your Web site, but you may need to promote a particular product or service of your own.

Or you might want to use a marquee to warn your visitors that a deadline is approaching—for example, the end of a benefits open-enrollment period or a fund-raising effort. With FrontPage, you can easily add a marquee and format it to your specific needs. Follow these steps:

1. With the Our Destinations page displayed on the Normal tab, click an insertion point at the end of the first paragraph and press Enter to start a new paragraph.

2. Choose Component and Marquee from the Insert menu to display this dialog box:

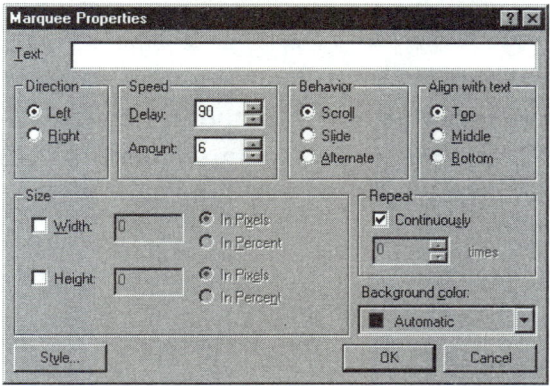

3. In the Text box, type *Hurry! Tours are booking up fast. Register soon!*

4. Change the Background Color setting to the green in the Theme Colors section. Then click OK.

5. Resize the marquee box until it is just wide enough to display its text.

6. Click the Preview tab to see the marquee in action.

Suppose you want the text to appear after the globe has spiraled onto the page and to scroll faster. Make the following adjustments:

1. Click the Normal tab. Then right-click the marquee box and choose Marquee Properties from the shortcut menu.

More marquee properties

You can use options in the Marquee Properties dialog box to specify the direction that the text moves, its alignment with the surrounding text, and how many times the marquee text is repeated. You can also change the type of motion used (the default is a scrolling motion). For example, select the Slide option to have the marquee text slide into view or select the Alternate option to have the text alternate between the scrolling and sliding options. To change the marquee's font, right-click it and choose Font from the shortcut menu. You can then adjust the font, size, color, and spacing between characters as necessary.

Specifying the delay →

2. In the Speed section, change the Delay setting to *420* to tell FrontPage to delay the appearance of the marquee text until 420 milliseconds after the page is displayed.

Specifying the speed →

3. Also in the Speed section, change the Amount setting from 6 to *24* to tell FrontPage to make the text move four times as fast. Then click OK.

4. Switch to the Preview tab again to test your changes.

You will probably want to experiment with marquees to come up with exactly the effect you want. If you want to add a banner advertisement to a page, see the tip below.

Adding a Hit Counter

If your Web server supports FrontPage Server Extensions, you might want to consider adding a component called a *hit counter* to your web's home page. The hit counter is automatically incremented each time someone displays the page in a Web browser and provides a running tally of how many visitors have checked out the page. This tally serves as a good indicator of how frequently your Web site is accessed and whether efforts to generate traffic on your site are having any effect. (See the tip on page 79 for information about ways to generate traffic on a commercial Web site.)

How hit counters work →

Let's add a hit counter to the bottom of the home page so that Exotic Excursions can keep track of how many people visit its site. Follow the steps on the facing page.

Using banner ads

If you want to advertise several products or services at a time, you may want to explore using a banner ad. A banner ad acts like a rotating billboard and displays a sequence of images in a certain time frame, separating each image with some sort of transition effect. To insert a banner ad, click the insertion point in the desired location and choose Component and then Banner Ad Manager from the Insert menu. For each image you want to display, click the Add button and select the image file. You can then rearrange or delete images using the adjacent buttons. Next select a transition effect from the Transition Effect drop-down list. To create a hyperlink from the banner ad, enter the address of the target in the Link To box. To change the size of the banner ad in pixels, change the Width and Height boxes. If you want to adjust the number of seconds each picture is displayed, change the setting in the Show Each Picture For edit box. Then click OK.

1. Display the home page (index.htm) on the Normal tab and then scroll to the bottom of the page.

2. Click an insertion point at the end of the *Return to Top* hyperlink and press Enter.

3. Click the Align Left button on the Formatting toolbar and then type *You are visitor number* and a space.

4. Choose Component and then Hit Counter from the Insert menu to display this dialog box:

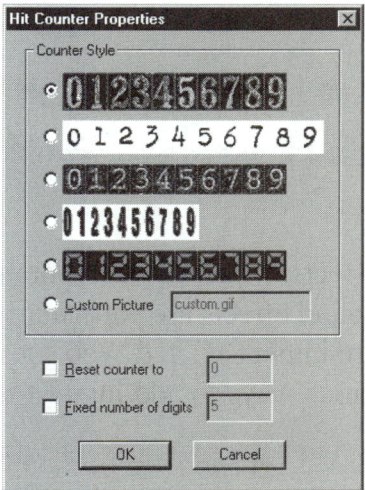

5. Select the fifth Counter Style option.

6. Click the Fixed Number Of Digits check box, change the setting to 6, and click OK. FrontPage inserts the placeholder *[Hit Counter]* at the insertion point, as shown on the next page.

Adding time stamps

Another component you can add to your web pages is a time stamp, which displays the time and/or date the page was last updated. Time stamps are useful for visitors who frequently check your site—if they see the date has not changed since their last visit, they know there is no new information available. To insert a time stamp, click an insertion point where you want the time stamp to appear (they usually appear at the bottom of a page). Next choose Date And Time from the Insert menu. In the Date And Time dialog box, specify the type of display and the format you want and click OK. If you want to change the text's font or size, simply select the text and adjust the formatting as usual.

Hit counter properties

You can use your own GIF-format graphic instead of one of FrontPage's predefined hit counter styles. To use a graphic, select the Custom Picture option and then type the location of the file. To reset the counter to 0 or set it to a different number, click the Reset Counter To check box and type the number you want to use.

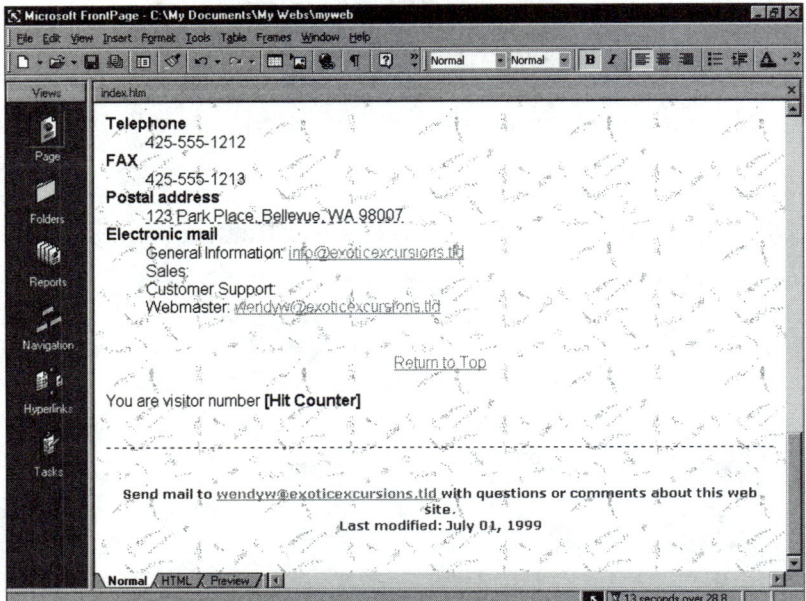

Using Sound Effects

In addition to visual special effects, you can incorporate sound effects into your pages. Sound effects are particularly effective for music or other entertainment-related Web sites, but they can also be used in various ways to add interest to other types of sites.

Inappropriate uses of sound

Bear in mind that in order for visitors to actually hear the sound, the browser they are using has to support sound effects, and they need the proper multimedia equipment. Unless you are confident that your visitors will be able to take advantage of the sound at your site, you probably shouldn't

Creating a table of contents

If your web is complex and contains several pages, you may want to include a table of contents. You can have FrontPage generate one automatically based on the navigation structure of your web. Visitors can then click any entry in the table of contents to move to that page. To create a table of contents, click an insertion point where you want it to appear and then choose Component and Table Of Contents from the Insert menu. In the Page URL For Starting Point edit box, enter the page you want to use as the starting point for the table of contents (usually the home page). Next select an option in the Heading Font Size drop-down list. To remove the starting page from the table of contents, select None. (You should select this option if your table of contents appears on the page you have designated as the starting page of the table.) You can also select options that tell FrontPage to show each page once, to display pages that have no incoming hyperlinks, and to automatically update the table of contents whenever any page in the web is edited. (You can also manually update a table of contents by opening and saving the page in which the table is located.)

use sound as a way of communicating important information. For example, if you want to include a speech by your organization's president or school's principal, you should display the text of the speech for everyone to see and include the option of listening to the speech for those people who have sound equipment.

For demonstration purposes, let's add a background sound to the home page of the Exotic Excursions web. You can use a sound file located on your hard drive, or you can use one of the sounds available on the Sounds tab of the Clip Art Gallery window. Follow these steps to use one of the sounds that comes with FrontPage:

1. Display the home page on the Normal tab of page view. Then right-click a blank area of the page and choose Page Properties from the shortcut menu to display this dialog box:

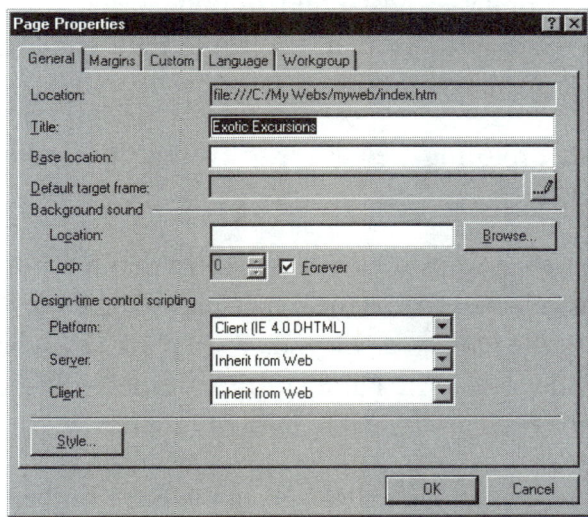

Adding a background sound

2. In the Background Sound section of the General tab, click the Location edit box and click the Browse button.

3. Click the Clip Art button in the bottom right corner of the dialog box to display the Sounds tab of the Clip Art Gallery.

4. Click the Music category to display the options shown on the next page. (If you don't see any clips, you can download sound files using a similar procedure to the one outlined on page 40 for graphics.)

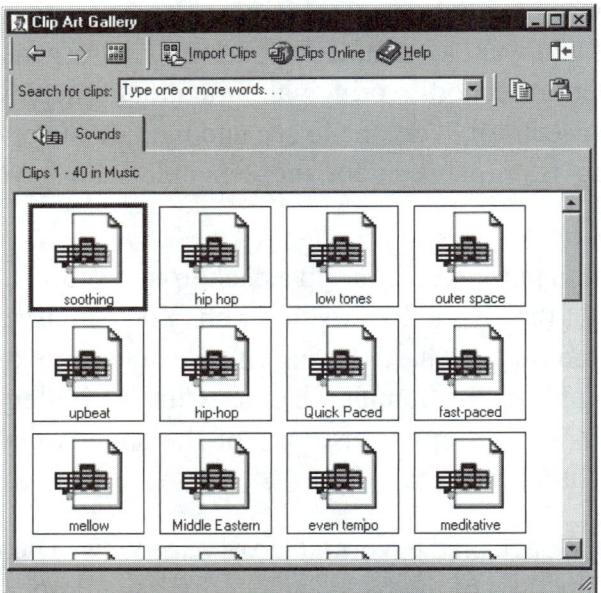

The Play Clip button

5. Select any icon to display the palette of buttons and then, assuming that your computer has sound equipment, click the Play Clip button to hear the sound. Close the Play window when you've heard enough.

6. When you finish exploring, select the Adventurous option and click Insert Clip.

7. Back in the Page Properties dialog box, verify that the Forever check box is selected so that the music plays in the background as long as the page is displayed. Then click OK. (To have the sound play a specific number of times, deselect the Forever check box and enter a value in the Loop box.)

Saving a sound as part of the web

8. Click the Save button and then click OK in the Save Embedded Files dialog box to add the sound to the list of files in the Myweb folder.

9. To hear the sound file, click the Preview tab. Then return to the Normal tab.

Adding Video

You can add video files to a Web site to show short "movies." Like sound effects, video effects are useful in entertainment-related Web sites, but they can also enhance other types of sites. For example, you could demonstrate a medical procedure or a lab procedure, or you could show a video testimonial from a satisfied customer who uses your product or service. Also like sound effects, you should be cautious about relying too heavily on video effects unless you know that your visitors' computers are equipped to handle them.

In addition to showing full-blown videos, you can also add animated graphics to your web's pages. Suppose you want to add a little animation to the Death Valley page of the Exotic Excursions web. As with sound files, you can use a video file located on your hard drive, or you can use one of the files available on the Motion Clips tab of the Clip Art Gallery window. Follow these steps:

1. Display the Death Valley page (serv02.htm) on the Normal tab in page view.

⬅ **Adding animated graphics**

2. With the insertion point located at the beginning of the *This is a brief description* placeholder paragraph, choose Picture and then Video from the expanded Insert menu.

3. In the Video dialog box, click the Clip Art button to display the Motion Clips tab of the Clip Art Gallery window.

4. Click the Nature category to display these clips:

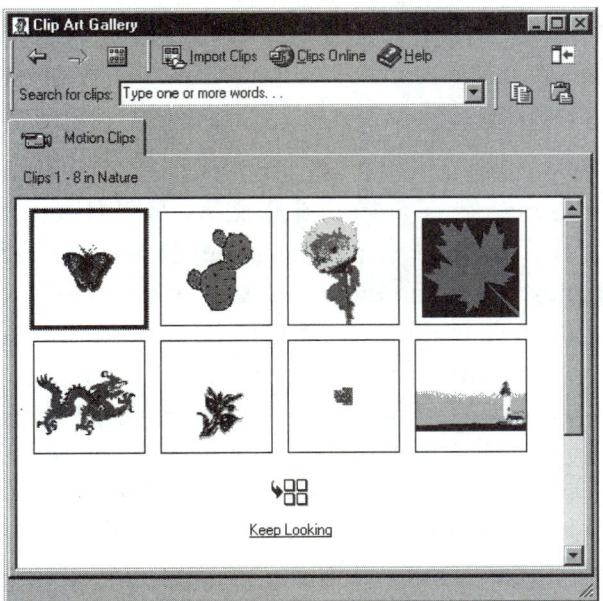

Again, you can download clips (see page 123).

Video properties

You can change how often a video you have added to a page is repeated and when it starts. Right-click the video file and choose Picture Properties from the shortcut menu. On the Video tab of the Picture Properties dialog box, change the Loop setting to adjust the number of times the video repeats or select Forever to have it play repeatedly. To adjust the amount of time in milliseconds between the showings of the video, change the Loop Delay setting. In the Start section of the dialog box, click either On File Open or On Mouse Over to specify when the video should start to play.

Previewing a clip

5. Click the cactus image and then click the Play Clip button. Watch the cactus as it blooms in the GIF Player window.

6. Close the GIF Player window, click the graphic, and click the Insert Clip button. FrontPage inserts the cactus graphic, which appears to be just like any other graphic you might insert from the Clip Art Gallery.

7. Press Enter and then make the graphic larger, as shown here:

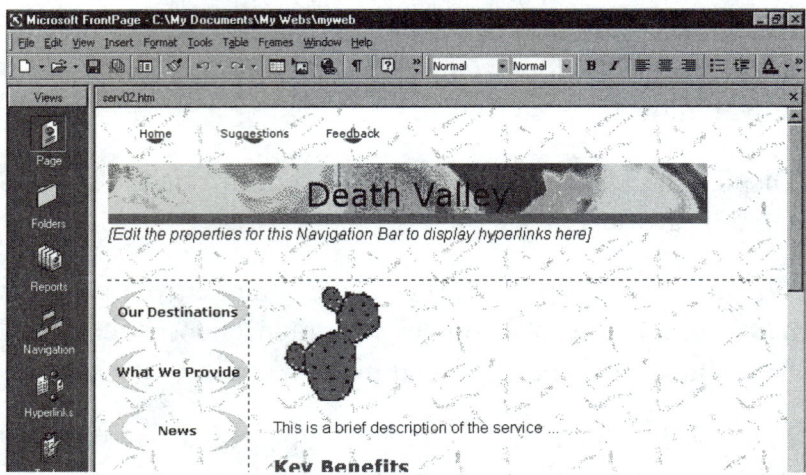

8. Save the graphic as part of the Exotic Excursions web.

With some video effects, you may have to wait until you publish the web to see the effect in action.

Working with Non-HTML Components

As you know, when you add text and images to your web in FrontPage, all the elements are controlled by HTML code. (You looked at this coding earlier on page 24.) However, there may be times when the elements you want to add to your web exceed the capabilities of HTML. At times like these, another option is to embed an *ActiveX control* or *Java applet* in your web page. Fortunately, you can add these non–HTML components in FrontPage without having to know the programming languages that created them. Unfortunately, some browsers don't support ActiveX and Java. So if your web is designed for the world in general, you should think carefully about embedding elements that some of your visitors may not be able to view.

In this section, we'll briefly show you how to add an ActiveX and a Java element to your web. It will then be up to you to decide how and when you want to use them.

Adding ActiveX Controls

ActiveX controls are small programs written in programming languages such as Microsoft Visual C++ and Microsoft Visual Basic. They perform specific functions, such as displaying calendars and stock tickers. You will find information about ActiveX on Microsoft's Web site, and you can download controls from several other locations.

As an example, suppose you want to add a calendar to the Our Destinations page so that visitors can check the dates of various tours. We download a calendar control from www.download.com/PC/ActiveX to give you a general idea of how you would add an ActiveX control to a page. Follow these steps, using any control you have available:

1. Display the Our Destinations page on the Normal tab and click an insertion point below the Resources hover button.

2. Choose Advanced and then ActiveX Control from the Insert menu to display the dialog box shown on the next page.

Downloading the latest controls

If you find that you need a control that is not currently available in the Select A Control list of the ActiveX Control dialog box, you can search for new ones. Microsoft continually introduces new ActiveX controls that you can download from the Microsoft Site Builder Network tools gallery. You can access this gallery at www.microsoft.com/gallery/samples/download. Whenever you download a new control, it is automatically added to the Select A Control list. Controls are removed from the list if you uninstall or delete them. To manage the Select A Control list, click the Customize button. Then click the check box next to any control that you want to make available and deselect the check box next to any control you don't want to be available. (This procedure modifies the display of the Select A Control list but does not actually install or delete ActiveX controls from your hard drive.)

Enabling/disabling ActiveX and Java

As well as specifying that you want your web to be compatible with certain browsers (see the tip on page 67), you can disable ActiveX and Java capabilities by choosing Page Options from the Tools menu. On the Compatibility tab, deselect the ActiveX Controls or Java Applets check boxes in the Technologies section to make any menu commands related to ActiveX or Java unavailable.

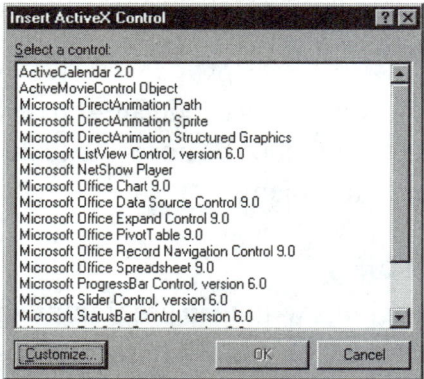

The Select A Control list displays all controls that are installed on your computer. (To install a new control or remove a control from the list, see the tip on the previous page.) If you are using Microsoft Office 2000, you can insert charts, pivot tables, and spreadsheets as well as controls.

3. Select the control you want to insert and click OK.

Now let's change the location of the control and set it off with a border. Follow these steps:

1. Right-click the control and choose ActiveX Control Properties from the shortcut menu. Then click the Object Tag tab to display the options shown below. (The options available in this dialog box may vary depending on the type of control you are working with.)

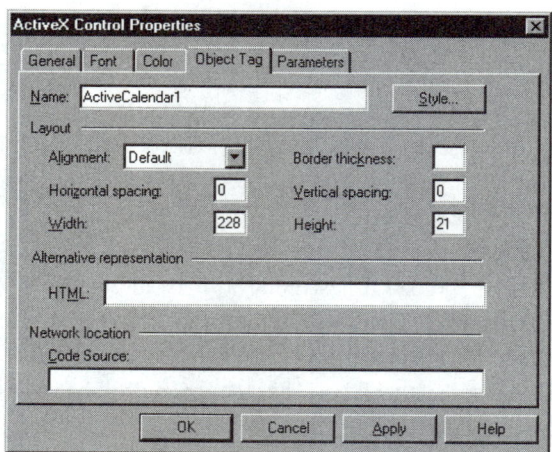

Chapter 5 Adding Special Effects

2. Change the Alignment setting to Center and enter *2* as the Border Thickness setting. Then click OK.

3. Save your changes and click the Preview tab to see how the control appears on the page. When we display the calendar, our control looks like this:

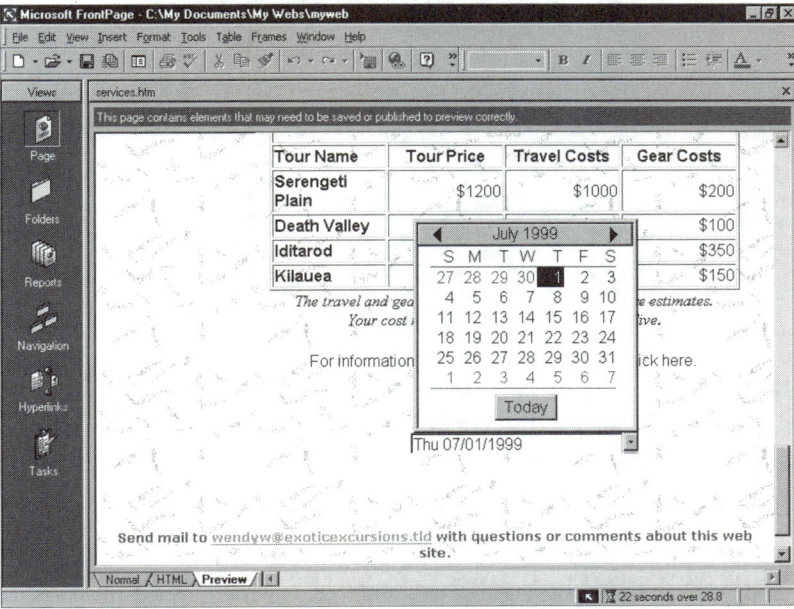

Adding Java Applets

As we already mentioned, Java applets are mini-programs created in the Java programming language that can be added to web pages to perform specific functions. If you have a Java applet you want to include in a FrontPage web, you can insert it with very little fuss. For example, on the Java Web site at www.javasoft.com, we found a clock. Here's how you would go about inserting this or a similar Java applet:

◄── The Java Web site

1. Click an insertion point where you want the applet to appear.

2. Choose Advanced and then Java Applet from the Insert menu to display the dialog box shown on the next page.

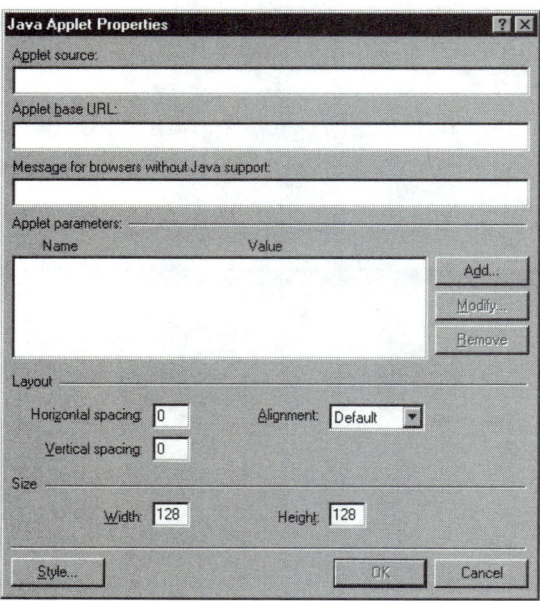

3. In the Applet Source box, type the name of the applet file. (Applet filenames have the extension *.class*.) If the file is stored in another folder, enter that folder's name in the Applet Base URL box.

4. In the Message For Browsers box, type the message you want any browser that does not support Java applets to display when visitors access this page.

5. If you need to add additional parameters in order for the Java applet to work, use the Applet Parameters section of the dialog box. (The documentation you download with the applet will tell you if any parameters are necessary.)

6. Finally, make any necessary adjustments to the applet's spacing, alignment, or size in the appropriate edit boxes. Then click OK.

Inserting plug-ins

With FrontPage, you can insert links to files that cannot be viewed with a Web browser but can be viewed using a "helper" program called a *plug-in*. For example, to make a PowerPoint presentation available through a Web page, you can insert a plug-in for the PowerPoint Viewer so that visitors who do not have PowerPoint on their computers can still display the presentation. To insert a plug-in, choose Advanced and then Plug-In from the Insert menu. In the Data Source edit box, enter the location of the plug-in. In the Message For Browsers edit box, enter text that is to be displayed if the browser can't display plug-ins. Next specify the settings you want for the size and layout of the plug-in and click OK.

After you insert the applet, you can edit its properties by right-clicking it and choosing Java Applet Properties from the shortcut menu.

In this chapter, we have given you a broad overview of the special effects that you can incorporate into your web's pages. As you continue to work with FrontPage, you will undoubtedly find new and unique ways to use special effects. Don't be afraid to experiment!

Maintaining and Updating a Web

You first work with the tasks list, which you use to keep track of your web's pages. Next you see how to document your web using comments and keep your site up-to-date using included pages, scheduled pages, and variables. Then you see how to update a published web.

The techniques covered in this chapter are important for the ongoing integrity of a Web site, particularly if you work with other people on its design and if it includes time-sensitive information.

Web pages created and concepts covered:

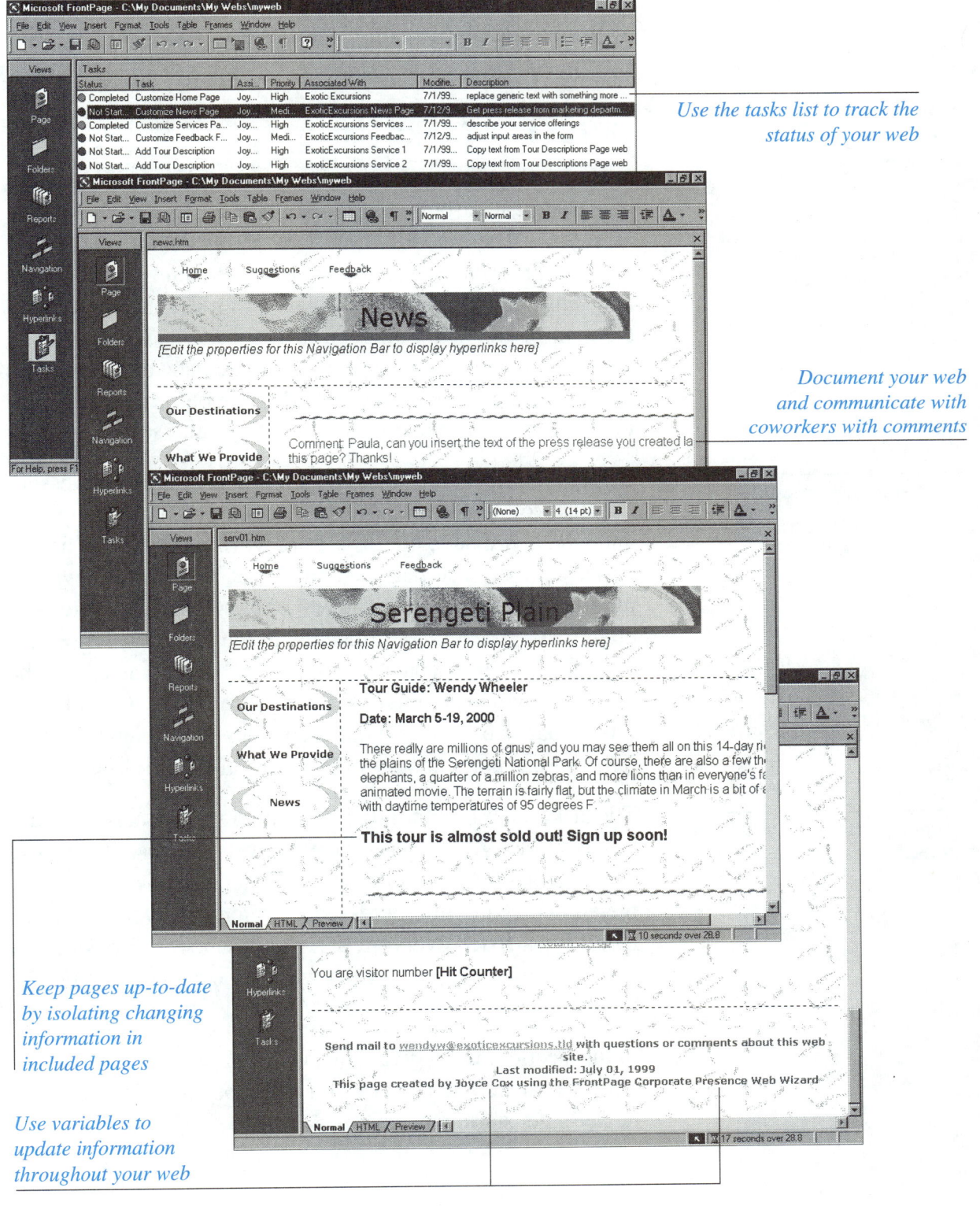

Use the tasks list to track the status of your web

Document your web and communicate with coworkers with comments

Keep pages up-to-date by isolating changing information in included pages

Use variables to update information throughout your web

In this chapter, we discuss issues relating to the ongoing maintenance of webs. First you take a closer look at tasks view, which allows you to track the various parts of your web and see their status at a glance. Then you look at ways to keep webs flexible and up-to-date as your needs or your information changes.

Using the Tasks List

Web development is not a linear process. You will rarely be able to start at the beginning and proceed in an orderly fashion until you come out with a finished product at the end. When you use FrontPage to create webs that contain several pages and multiple components, you are often developing several elements at the same time, weaving back and forth among them. You may insert a hyperlink in one page and then jump to the target page to do some work there before coming back to develop another part of the first page, and so on.

Tracking development

Because of the nature of this development process, it is essential that you keep track of which tasks you have completed and which you have not. If you are working alone and have a great memory, you may be able to get by without a written record of your progress. The rest of us will need a more concrete way of keeping all the balls in the air. By using FrontPage's tasks list, you can monitor what still needs to be accomplished in an organized way, without the risk of losing bits of paper or having your web tasks buried among other items in a generic hand-written or electronic to-do list.

Communicating among team members

The tasks list is particularly important if you are part of a team that is working together to create a web, because it acts as a sort of collective memory about which tasks have been completed, which are in progress, and which have yet to be tackled. It can also tell everyone at a glance who is responsible for completing which parts of the web and which tasks have the highest priority.

In this section, we'll give you an overview of the tasks list so that you can decide whether you might be able to make use of it. Let's get started:

1. If necessary, start FrontPage and open the home page of the Exotic Excursions web located in the Myweb folder.

2. Next click the Tasks icon in the Views bar to display the web in tasks view, as shown here:

Displaying the tasks list

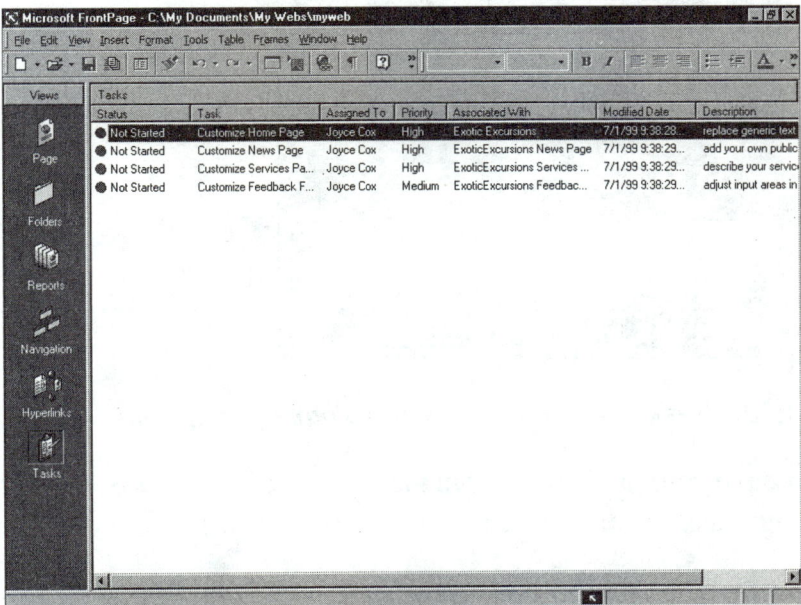

As you may recall, FrontPage automatically associated these four tasks with the pages created by the Corporate Presence Wizard way back in Chapter 1. For each task, this view has columns for its status, its name, who the task has been assigned to, its priority level, the file associated with the task, when the task was last worked on (modified), and a description of the task.

Creating Tasks

The four default tasks definitely need to be performed for any new web of this type, but to take advantage of tasks view, you will undoubtedly want to add tasks that are specific to the web you are building. Back on page 83 in Chapter 4, you experimented with frames pages in a separate web called Tour Descriptions Page. Suppose you want to remind yourself to copy the descriptions you entered for the individual tours in that web to the appropriate pages of the Exotic Excursions web. Follow the steps on the next page to record this task.

1. Click the arrow to the right of the New button on the Standard toolbar and select Task from the drop-down list. FrontPage displays this dialog box:

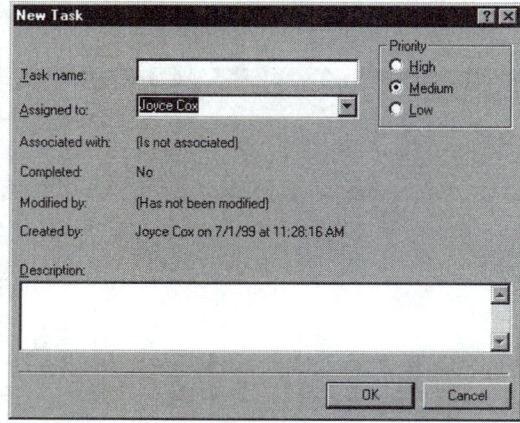

2. In the Task Name box, type *Add Tour Descriptions*.

3. Leave your name entered in the Assigned To edit box. (To assign tasks to others, see the tip on page 140.)

4. In the Description box, type *Copy text from Tour Descriptions Page web*.

Assigning a priority level

5. In the Priority section, click the High option. Then click OK. FrontPage adds the new task to the bottom of the list.

6. To widen the Description column so that you can see all its text, point to the right border of the Modified Date column's header, and drag to the left.

7. Repeat step 6 for some of the other columns, until the tasks list looks something like this:

Column width shortcut

If you want to quickly adjust the width of a column to fit its longest entry, you can double-click the right border of the column's header.

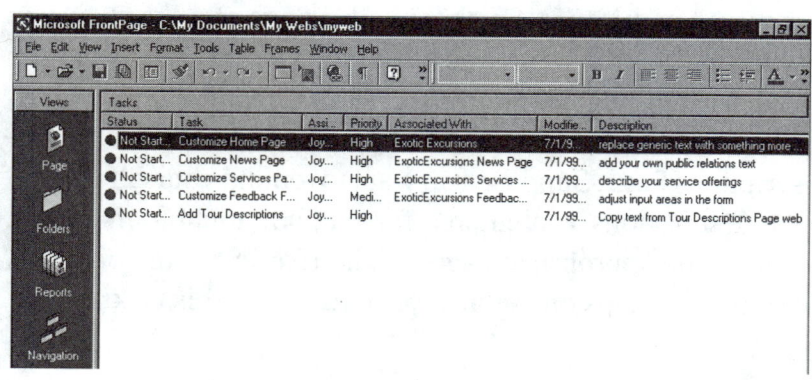

As you can see, the new task is not associated with a specific file because more than one file is involved. To associate a task with a file, you need to create the task in a different view, like this:

1. Switch to page view and then open the Serengeti Plain page (serv01.htm).

   ← **Associating a file with a task**

2. Choose New and then Task from the File menu to display the New Task dialog box.

3. Type *Add Tour Description* as the task name and *Copy text from Tour Descriptions Page web* as the description. Then set the priority to High and click OK.

4. Repeat steps 1 through 3 to create similar tasks for the Death Valley, Iditarod, and Kilauea pages.

5. When you finish, click the Tasks icon to switch back to tasks view, where you see these results:

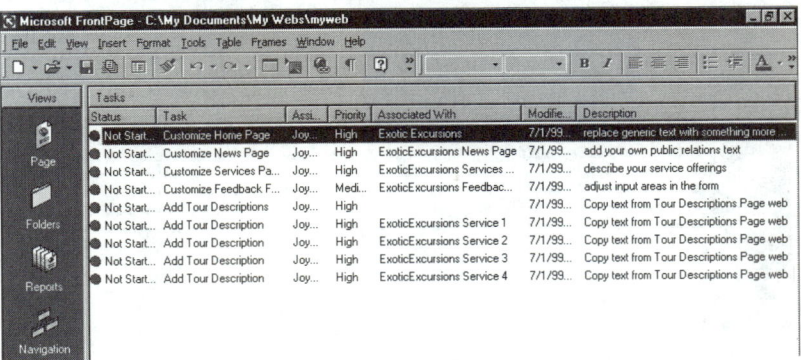

Editing Tasks

Like any other to-do list, your FrontPage task list will change over time as you complete some chores and add some new ones. Suppose you want to record that you have completed some of the tasks associated with the Exotic Excursions web. You also want to delete the extraneous Add Tour Descriptions entry. Follow these steps:

1. Right-click the Customize Home Page task at the top of the list and choose Mark As Completed from the shortcut menu. FrontPage changes the Status column to *Completed*, replaces

Sorting tasks

To sort the tasks in the tasks list, you can click the header for any column. For example, to sort the tasks based on their priority, click the header for the priority column. Click the header again to reverse the order of the sort.

the red dot with a green dot, and changes the date and/or time in the Modified column.

2. Repeat the previous step to mark the Customize Services Page task as complete.

3. Now change the priority and description of the Customize News Page task. Right-click the task and choose Edit Task from the shortcut menu to display a Task Details dialog box that is similar to the New Task dialog box shown earlier on page 136.

4. Change the priority to Medium and replace the Description text with *Get press release from marketing department*. Then click OK.

Deleting tasks

5. Next select the Add Tour Descriptions task (the one that is not associated with a particular file). Press the Delete key and then click Yes to confirm the deletion. Here are the results:

You can also make editing changes to tasks directly in the list by selecting the task you want to change, clicking the entry you want to modify, and then entering your changes.

Working on Tasks

Switching among views and displaying pages are relatively simple processes in FrontPage. However, if you are diligent about keeping up with your tasks list and find yourself reviewing it often, you may find it useful to be able to jump directly to the page associated with a task so that you can begin working on it immediately. This method not only saves time

Displaying/hiding completed tasks

If you return to tasks view and notice that FrontPage is not displaying completed tasks, the Show Task History command is not turned on. To display completed tasks, right-click a blank area of the tasks view window and choose Show Task History from the shortcut menu to toggle it on. If you decide you don't want to view completed tasks, simply choose the command again to toggle it off.

but also enables you to keep the tasks list up-to-date more efficiently, as you'll see if you follow these steps:

1. First right-click the Add Tour Description task for the Exotic Excursions Service 1 page and choose Start Task from the shortcut menu. FrontPage displays the Serengeti Plain page in page view.

2. Next open the Tour Descriptions Page web by choosing Open Web from the File menu, clicking the My Documents icon, and double-clicking the My Webs folder. Then select Myweb2 and click the Open button. You now have two instances of FrontPage running on your computer: an inactive instance that displays the Exotic Excursions web, and an active instance that displays the Tour Descriptions Page web.

   Running two instances of FrontPage

3. In the active Tour Descriptions Page web, open the folder list, double-click serengeti_plain.htm to display the Serengeti Plain page, and then close the folder list. Your screen now looks like this:

4. Select the Tour Guide and Date lines and the descriptive paragraph and click the Copy button on the Standard toolbar.

> **Creating tasks for other file types**
>
> If your web contains files such as spreadsheets or word processing files, you can create tasks that are linked to those files. First display the folder list and select the file for which you want to create a task. Next choose New and then Task from the File menu to display the New Task dialog box. Because you selected a file before creating the new task, FrontPage associates the task with that file. When you start a task linked to another file type, FrontPage opens the file in its associated program.

5. Next activate the Serengeti Plain page in the Exotic Excursions web and then select the placeholder text in the opening paragraph.

6. Click the Paste button on the Standard toolbar.

7. Delete the *Key Benefits* heading and the bulleted list below it. Here are the results:

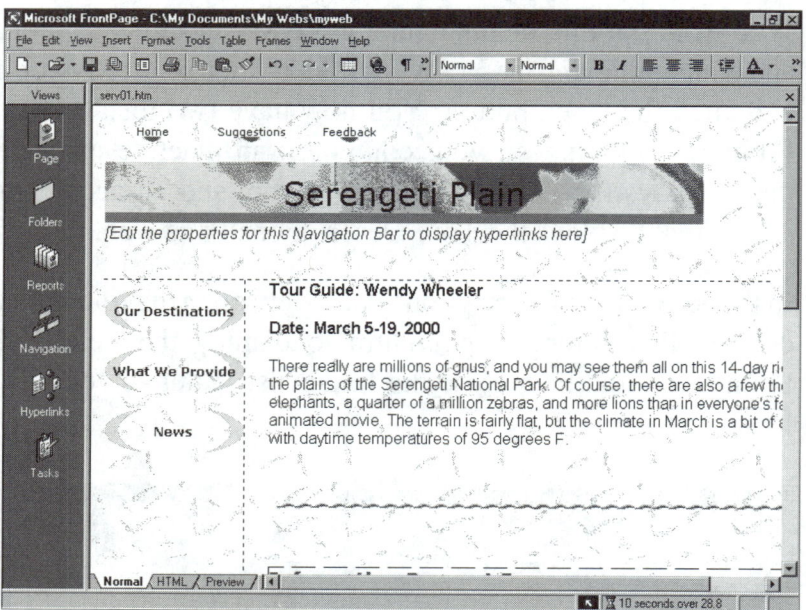

8. Click the Save button to update the page. FrontPage displays the message box shown at the top of the facing page.

Assigning tasks and files

If you work in a networked environment and are part of a team that is working on a web, you can assign tasks to other members of your workgroup. When creating a new task, click the arrow to the right of the Assigned To edit box and select a name from the drop-down list. If the name you want to use does not appear on the list, simply type the name. (It will then be added to the Assigned To list.) To assign an existing task to someone else, right-click the task, choose Edit Task from the shortcut menu, and then select a name in the Task Details dialog box. In reports view, you can assign a specific file to a workgroup member. Switch to reports view and select the Assigned To report in the Reports drop-down list. You can then click the Assigned To column of any file and select a name from the list. To assign multiple files to one person simultaneously, first select the necessary files by clicking each filename while holding down the Ctrl key. Right-click the selection and choose Properties from the shortcut menu. Display the Workgroup tab and then select the name you want from the Assigned To drop-down list. (If you need to make changes to the Assigned To list, see the tip on the facing page.)

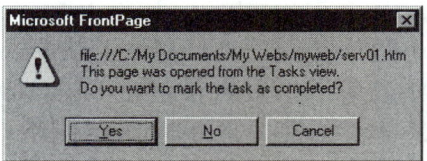

9. Click Yes to mark the task complete. (Obviously, FrontPage has no way of knowing exactly what you did to the Serengeti Plain page, so it cannot automatically mark the task for you.)

10. Return to tasks view to check that FrontPage has properly updated the list.

11. Repeat the previous steps to copy the descriptions of the three remaining tours from the Tour Descriptions Page web to the Exotic Excursions web. (Be sure to open each page from tasks view so that you can have FrontPage update the tasks list when you complete the task. Otherwise, you will have to update the list manually.)

12. Before moving on, close the second instance of FrontPage by activating its window and clicking its Close button.

Keeping a Web Site Up-to-Date

In Chapter 5, we showed you how to insert several components in the Exotic Excursions web by choosing their respective commands from the Components submenu of the Insert menu. In this section, we introduce a few components that can help streamline the process of keeping your web up-to-date. You'll see how to communicate with other people who are working on the web, how to include pages or images that will change or disappear after a certain date, and how to automatically update an item of information that appears throughout your site.

Documenting a Web with Comments

You might be developing a web under a variety of circumstances. For example, you might be working in splendid isolation with complete control over every element on every page. Or you might have been delegated responsibility for

Modifying the Assigned To list

As discussed in the tip on the facing page, you can assign tasks or specific files in your webs to members of your workgroup (or to an entire workgroup). To add a new name to the Assigned To list, you can type the name when assigning the task or file. You can also right-click any file in reports view and choose Properties from the shortcut menu. Next display the Workgroup tab and click the Names button to display the Usernames Master List dialog box. To add a new name, simply enter the name in the New Username box and then click Add. To delete a name, select a name from the list and click Delete. To return the list to its previous configuration, click Reset. Then click OK twice to close both dialog boxes.

Reasons for documentation

just one page of a web that is being developed by a team of contributors. Regardless of the circumstances, you will want to document your efforts so that when you return to a page in the future or a colleague takes over your web responsibilities, a clear record is available about the page's status, design decisions, potential future developments, and so on. The easiest way to document your web pages is with comments.

When you insert a comment in a page, the text is visible when you or another member of your development team views the page in FrontPage, but not when visitors view the page in a Web browser. You can insert comments during the various development phases as an audit trail or to communicate with team members. You can also insert comments after the Web site is up and running on a server.

As an example, suppose you are working with Paula Pedals from the Exotic Excursions marketing department on the web's News page and you decide to leave her a message on the page about its content. Follow these steps:

1. With the tasks list displayed, right-click the Customize News Page task and choose Start Task from the shortcut menu.

2. On the News page, click an insertion point between the wavy line and the placeholder heading and choose Comment from the Insert menu to display this dialog box:

3. In the Comment box, type *Paula, can you insert the text of the press release you created last month on this page? Thanks!* Then click OK. FrontPage inserts the comment using the font settings applied to the paragraph containing the insertion point, as shown on the facing page.

Chapter 6 Maintaining and Updating a Web

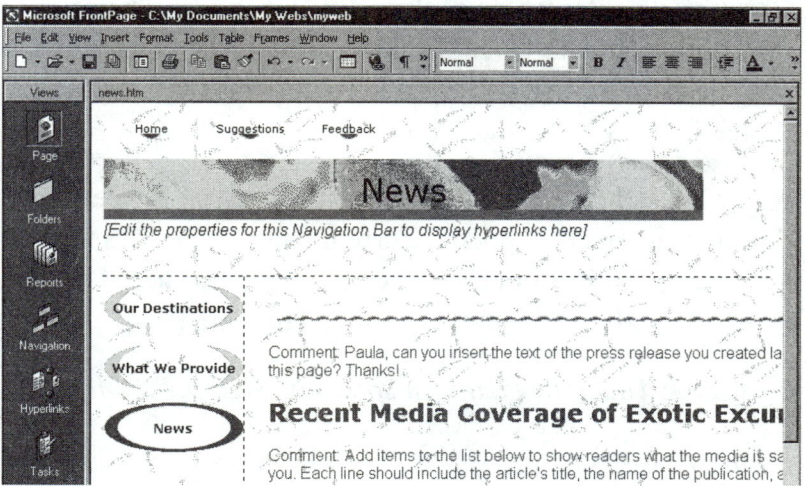

4. Save the page, clicking No when FrontPage asks whether it should mark the task as complete.

5. Click the Preview tab to check that the comment will not be visible to your visitors, and then return to the Normal tab.

To edit the comment, you can simply double-click it to redisplay the Comment dialog box. When Paula has made her contribution to this page, she can delete the comment by selecting it and pressing Delete.

Editing comments

Using an Include Page

Often, you will want several pages (or even all the pages) of a web to display information that you expect to change at some time in the future. Examples are lists of events or other time-sensitive announcements, special offers, trademark and copyright information, survey results, and so on. With FrontPage, you create a separate page containing the changing information and then embed, or include, it in the pages where you want the information to appear. When the time comes to update the information, you have to edit and save only one page and instantly the information is updated on every page where you included it.

Types of information that change

For demonstration purposes, let's create a page that displays a warning when a tour is almost booked to capacity:

1. Click the New Page button on the toolbar to create a new, blank page in the Exotic Excursions web.

Removing a theme from a page

2. Right-click a blank area of the page and choose Theme from the shortcut menu. Click the Selected Page(s) option, select No Theme in the list, and click OK to turn off the Citrus Punch theme for this particular page.

3. Right-click the page again and choose Shared Borders from the shortcut menu. Click the Current Page option, deselect the Top, Left, and Bottom check boxes so that no shared borders are displayed on this page, and then click OK.

4. Next type *This tour is almost sold out! Sign up soon!*

5. Select the text, change its size to 4 (14 pt), and make it bold.

6. Save the page in the Myweb folder, with both a page title and a filename of *Availability*.

Now let's include this new page in two of the tour pages. Follow these steps:

1. Display the Serengeti Plain page (serv01.htm).

2. With the insertion point below the description paragraph, choose Component and then Include Page from the Insert menu to display this dialog box:

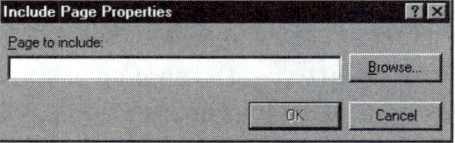

Specifying the page

3. Click the Browse button, double-click the Availability page in the list of files to display it in the Page To Include box, and click OK. The results are shown at the top of the facing page.

Creating subwebs

If you know that one part of your web is likely to change, you can isolate that part as a discreet unit called a subweb. You can also use subwebs to reflect the organizational structure of a company. For example, a company web might include a home page with links to subwebs for each department. You create a subweb by choosing New and then Web from the File menu in the usual way, but you specify that the subweb should be created in a subfolder of the parent web's folder. See the tip on page 152 for information about publishing subwebs.

Chapter 6 Maintaining and Updating a Web   145

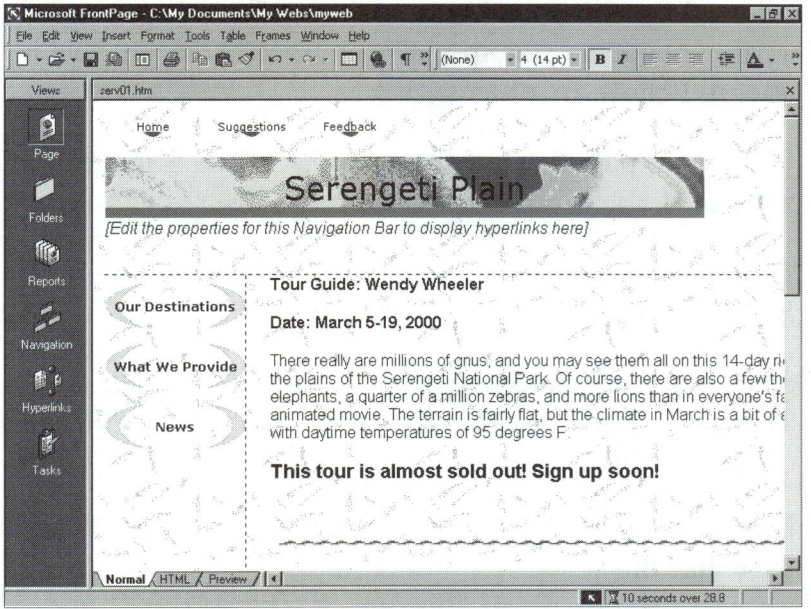

4. Save the page.

5. Next display the Kilauea page and include the Availability page in the same location. Then save that page.

Changing an Include Page

Suppose you receive word that these two tours are now completely sold out. You need to edit the Availability page so that the tour pages display the updated information. Try this:

1. With the Kilauea page displayed, right-click the text of the included page and choose the Open File command from the shortcut menu.

2. Change the text to read *Sorry, this tour is completely sold out!* and click the Save button.

3. Return to the Kilauea page and check that the text has been properly updated. Then check the Serengeti Plain page.

Using a Scheduled Include Page

A scheduled included page works the same way as a regular included page except that you can designate a date after which the page should no longer be displayed. Suppose the Iditarod tour has not been selling very well and you want to offer a special discount for cyclists who sign up for the tour

Using scheduled graphics

In addition to scheduling a page to be included in another page at a specified time, you can schedule a graphic image. Click an insertion point where you want the image to appear and choose Component and then Scheduled Picture from the Insert menu. Then select options in the Scheduled Picture Properties dialog box as you do in the steps on the next page.

before December 31, 1999. You can tell FrontPage to display a page announcing the special offer through that date but not after it. Follow these steps:

1. Open a new page that has no theme and whose shared borders are turned off.

2. Type *Sign up before December 31, 1999 and receive a 10% early-bird discount!*

3. Select the text, change the size to 4 (14 pt), and make it bold. Then save the page with a title of *Special Offer* and a filename of *Special_Offer*.

Now you can include the Special Offer page on the Iditarod page, like this:

1. Display the Iditarod page (serv03.htm).

Specifying the schedule

2. With the insertion point below the tour description paragraph, choose Component and then Scheduled Include Page from the Insert menu to display this dialog box:

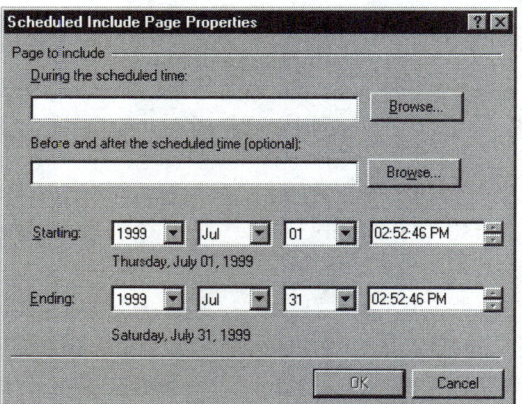

3. Click the Browse button next to the During The Scheduled Time box and double-click the Special Offer page. (To display a different page or graphic before and after the scheduled time, enter the file you want to use in the Before And After The Scheduled Time box.)

4. In the Starting section, change the date to *April 1, 1999*. In the Ending section, select *January 1, 2000* as the date and *12:00:01 AM* as the time. Then click OK.

5. Depending on the current date, you might see the Special Offer page on the Iditarod page, or you might see an Expired Scheduled Include Page placeholder. If you see the placeholder, go back and enter different dates in the Starting and Ending sections of the Scheduled Include Page Properties dialog box so that FrontPage displays the included page.

6. Save the Iditarod page.

Working with Variables

When you create a web, FrontPage automatically records important information such as the author's name and the web's URL. Although the same items are recorded each time, the content, or *value*, of the items varies from web to web, so items of information like these are called *variables*. For example, the author's name variable for a web produced on one computer might be Sandy Spokes, and the author's name variable for different web produced on another computer might be Gary Gears.

Often you determine what values are assigned to the variables used in your webs. For example, when you first created the Exotic Excursions web in Chapter 1, FrontPage took items of information that you entered in the wizard's dialog boxes and recorded them as variables. It then plugged the variables into specific areas of your web's pages. As a result, you did not need to type the Exotic Excursions e-mail addresses, mailing address, or phone numbers on the home page because FrontPage had already done that job for you.

Variables are an extremely useful way of working with information that might change. You can define a value that is used on several pages of a web as a variable and then change the variable to have the corresponding information change wherever the variable is used. As a demonstration, follow these steps to add a variable and change its definition:

1. Display the home page and scroll to the bottom.

2. Click an insertion point at the end of the *Last modified* paragraph in the bottom shared border and then press Shift+Enter to start a new line.

3. Type *This page created by:* and a space.

Inserting variables

4. Choose Component and then Substitution from the Insert menu to display this dialog box:

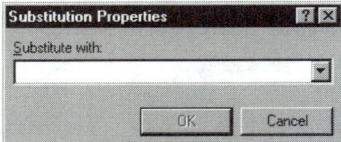

5. Click the arrow to the right of the Substitute With edit box and select Author from the drop-down list. Then click OK. FrontPage inserts the name assigned to your computer or the name entered when the program was installed on your computer.

6. Type a space, then the words *using the*, and another space.

7. Insert the GeneratedBy variable, which displays how the page was created.

8. Click a blank area of the page to see these results:

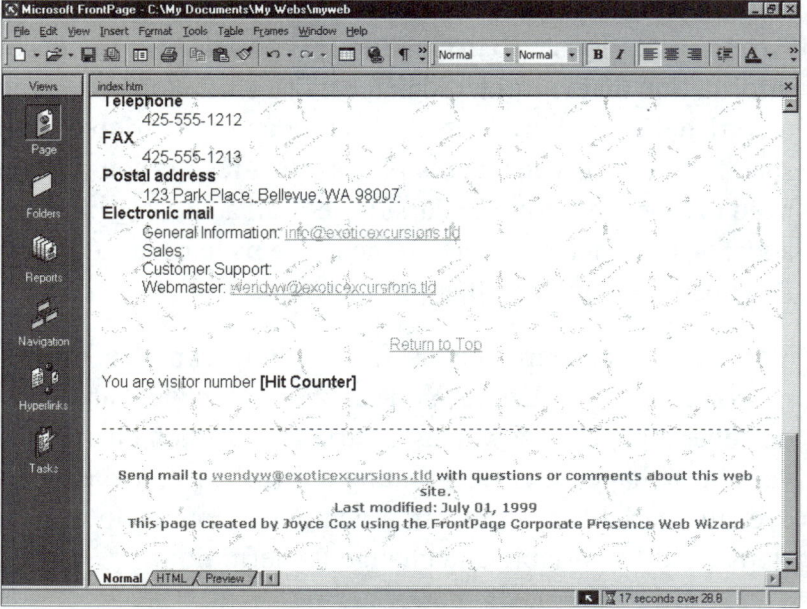

Chapter 6 Maintaining and Updating a Web   149

9. Save your changes.

    Suppose the area code for Exotic Excursions has changed from *425* to *428*. If the phone and fax numbers appear on several pages throughout the web, updating them all would take quite awhile. However, if the phone and fax numbers were inserted as variables (as they are on the home page of the Exotic Excursions web), updating them couldn't be easier. Follow these steps:

1. Choose Web Settings from the Tools menu and then click the Parameters tab to display these options:

    Updating variables

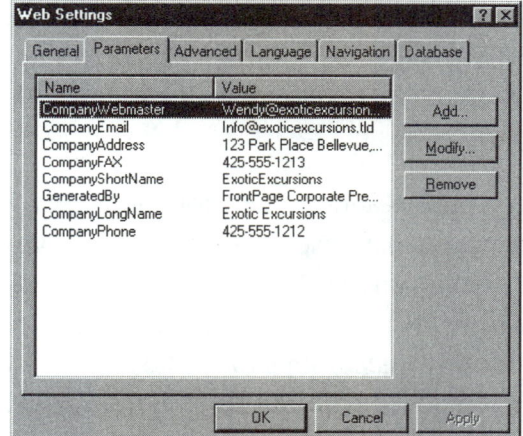

    FrontPage displays the list of variables it created when you first set up the web and shows the value you assigned to each variable.

2. Select the CompanyFAX variable and click the Modify button to display this dialog box:

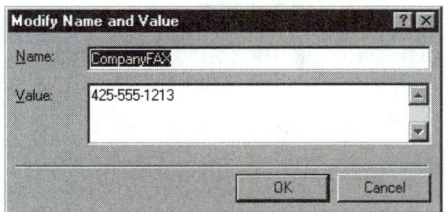

3. In the Value box, replace *425* with *428* and click OK.

Creating new variables

You are not restricted to the list of variables provided by FrontPage. To create your own variable, choose Web Settings from the Tools menu and click the Parameters tab. Click the Add button and type a name for the variable in the Name box. Enter the value you want to assign to the variable in the Value box and click OK. FrontPage then adds the new variable to the list on the Parameters tab. To remove a variable from this list, select the variable and click the Remove button. Then simply click OK.

The Refresh button

4. Repeat steps 2 and 3 to update the area code for the Company-Phone variable. Then click OK in the Web Settings dialog box to return to your page.

5. To update the variables, choose Refresh from the View menu or click the Refresh button on the Standard toolbar. FrontPage then displays the new area codes.

Publishing New Web Pages

In Chapter 3, we walked you through the steps for publishing an entire web on a Web server. Once your web is up and running, either on the World Wide Web or on an intranet, you will undoubtedly need to update existing pages and add new ones from time to time. If your Web server has FrontPage Server Extensions installed, you can easily keep all the components of your Web site current.

Suppose Exotic Excursions has added a new tour to its roster. You need to add a new page that describes this tour and you need to update the list of tours on the Our Destinations page to include it. Then you need to publish the new and updated pages on your server. Follow these steps to see how to create the tour page and add a link to it on the Our Destinations page:

1. Display the Our Destinations page (services.htm) and scroll the last tour (Kilauea) into view.

2. Click an insertion point after *To the Brink and Back* and press Enter.

3. Type *Amazon Rain Forest*, press Enter twice, type *Pedal beside the Piranha*, and press Enter again.

4. Format the heading and motto to look like all the others.

5. If you want, go ahead and find a suitable graphic to insert to the left of the new tour's heading.

Next you need to create the new page and link it to the Our Destinations page, which you can do very efficiently in FrontPage. Try the steps on the facing page.

1. On the Our Destinations page, select the new tour's heading.

2. Click the Hyperlink button, and then click the Create A Page And Link To The New Page button to the right of the URL box. FrontPage displays the New dialog box.

3. Check that the Normal Page icon is selected and click OK.

4. With the new page displayed, type the following, pressing Enter after each paragraph:

   Tour Guide: Wendy Wheeler

   Date: September 3-31, 2000

   Join us for our inaugural ride along the Amazon River, through the world's largest rain forest. In four weeks, you'll cover 1700 miles (almost half the length of the river). Along the way, you'll encounter groups of indigenous peoples, as well as more species of plants and animals than anywhere else on earth. The challenge? Narrow tracks, a humid climate, and the piranha!

5. Make the first two lines bold.

6. Save the page with *Amazon Rain Forest* as the page title and *serv05* as the filename.

   Now follow these steps to update the web's navigation structure so that it includes the new page:

1. Switch to navigation view and display the folder list.

2. Drag the serv05.htm file over the child pages of the Our Destinations box, releasing the mouse button when the new box appears to the right of the Kilauea box.

3. Turn off the folder list and return to page view, where FrontPage displays the new page with its updated banner.

4. If necessary, turn on the left navigation bar by choosing Shared Borders from the Format menu, clicking the Current Page option, clicking the Left check box, and clicking OK. The page now looks as shown on the next page.

Updating the navigation structure

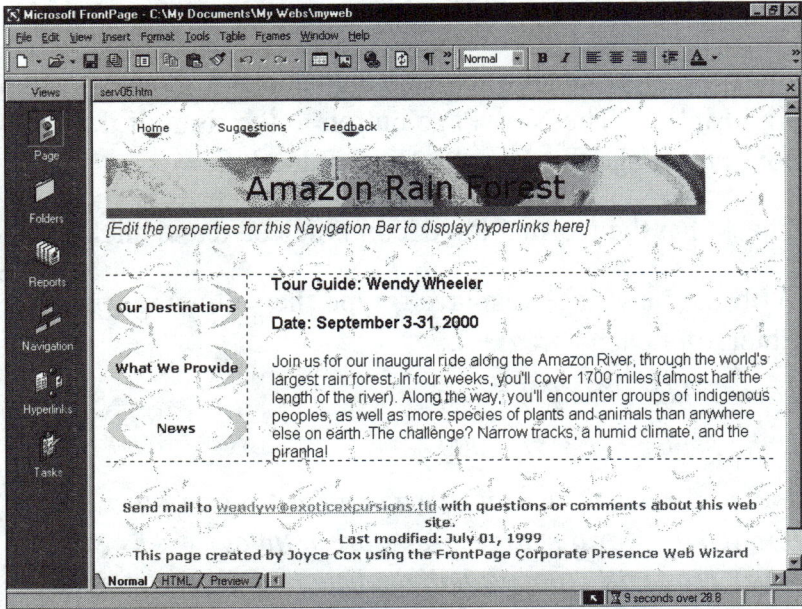

5. Display the Our Destinations page and scroll to the top. The new tour has been added to the child-page hyperlinks on the navigation bar below the banner, as you can see here:

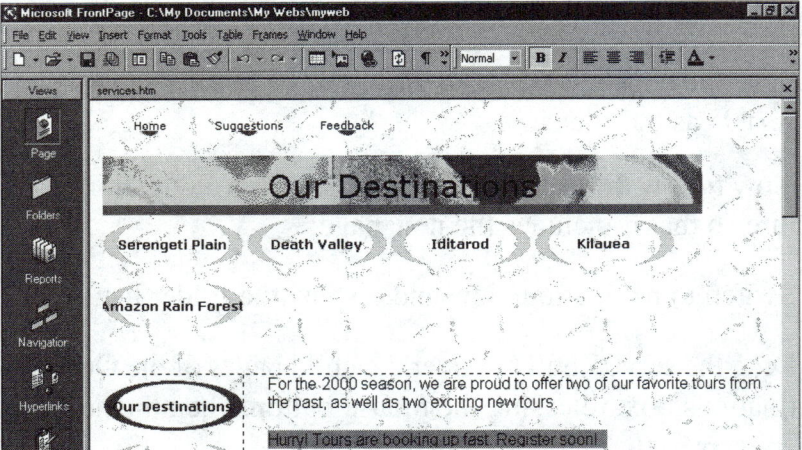

> **Other publishing options**
>
> In the Publish Web dialog box, there are two additional options you can select. If you click the Include Subwebs check box, FrontPage will publish all subwebs of the current web. If you know that you are publishing your web to a secure port of a Web server that supports Secure Sockets Layer (SSL), you should click the Secure Connection Required check box. (Your Webmaster or ISP will be able to give you more information about this option.)

Now you are ready to publish the new tour page and the modified Our Destinations page. Follow these steps:

1. Save all the open pages that have changes. (They're marked with an asterisk on the Window menu.)

2. Choose Publish Web from the File menu to display the dialog box shown earlier on page 70.

3. Click the Options button to display these options:

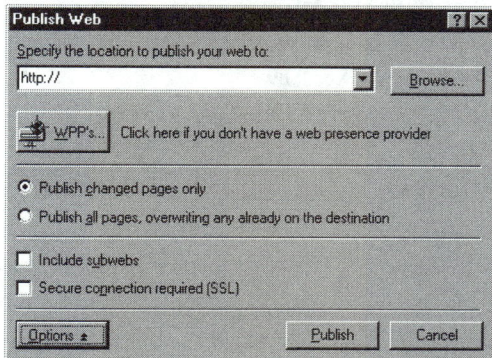

4. Enter the URL of your Web server in the Specify The Location To Publish Your Web To box.

5. To publish only the new or changed pages, click the Publish Changed Pages Only option. To publish all the pages in the web so that the version located on your computer overwrites the one on the server, click the Publish All Pages option.

6. You aren't actually going to send these files right now, so click Cancel instead of clicking Publish.

That ends our discussion of how to maintain and update the webs you create in FrontPage. Along with the skills you acquired in the previous chapters, you are now well-equipped to create unique and powerful webs. Don't be afraid to keep experimenting!

Publishing only specified pages

If you are still working on your web and you don't want to publish certain pages that are still under construction, you can tell FrontPage not to publish them. Switch to reports view and select Publish Status from the Reports drop-down list on the Reporting toolbar. Select the file(s) you don't want to publish, right-click the selection, and then choose Properties from the shortcut menu. On the Workgroup tab, select the Exclude This File When Publishing The Rest Of The Web check box at the bottom of the dialog box. Then click OK. FrontPage displays *Don't Publish* in the Publish column of the report. To later mark a file so that it will be published, simply deselect the check box on the Workgroup tab. To quickly designate the publishing status of a particular file, select it from the folder list, right-click, and choose Properties from the shortcut menu.

Deleting published pages

Once you have published a web, you may need to periodically delete old files to keep the web up-to-date. To do so, simply delete the file(s) as usual on your own computer. Then publish the updated web to the server as outlined in the above steps. Click Yes when FrontPage asks if you want to delete the same files from the Web server that you've just deleted from your computer.

Index

A

absmiddle alignment 39
activating open pages 42
ActiveX controls 126, 127
adding pages 18
addresses of Web servers 69
Advanced/ActiveX Control
  command 127
Advanced/Java Applet command 129
Advanced/Plug-in command 130
aligning
  graphics
    absmiddle 39
    right 37
  tables 92
  text 26
All Categories button 35
anchors 50
animated
  graphics 125, 126
  objects 114
animating graphics 114
Answer Wizard tab (Help
  window) 30
assigning tasks 140
audience, defining 79
automatic spell-checking 58

B

Back button 35
background
  page, changing 41
  sounds 123
banner ads 120
bars
  menu 6
  navigation 21, 51
    adding 52
    organizing buttons on 53
    reformatting 53
    renaming buttons 54
    updating 52
  status 6
  title 6
  tool. *See* toolbars
  Views 6
    Folders icon 16
    Hyperlinks icon 62
    Navigation icon 16
    Page icon 6
    Reports icon 64
    Tasks icon 15, 135
Bevel button 110
blank pages, creating 143

blinking text 25
Bookmark command 50
Bookmark Properties command
  (shortcut menu) 50
bookmarks 50
borders
  around graphics 110
  shared 26, 51
    turning on/off 54, 144
  around tables
    turning on/off 93
breaks, line 26
brightness/contrast of graphics,
  adjusting 108
browsers, Web xii
  designing for 67
bulleted lists 26
bullets 28
Bullets button 27
buttons
  form, creating 100
  Help, in dialog boxes 29
  hover 116
    adding graphics/sound 116
    formatting 117
    testing 118
  hyperlink 21
  navigation bar 52
    organizing 53
    renaming 54
  toolbar 8
    displaying hidden 9

C

capital letters, initial 15
Caption Properties command (shortcut
  menu) 94
captions, table 93
cascading style sheets 42
cells 91
  deleting 91, 97
  joining 93
Center button 26
centering
  table entries 93
  text 26
checking
  hyperlinks 62
  spelling 58
child pages 16
choosing commands 6
Circular Hotspot button 112
clip art. *See* graphics
Clip Art Gallery 34
Clip Gallery Live Web site 40

Clips Online button 40
Close Web command 89
closing
  FrontPage 31
  webs 89
collapsing webs 16
collecting data from forms 103
color
  of font, changing 25
  of hyperlinks 45
columns
  in tables
    changing width of 91
    deleting 91
    inserting 91
    moving 92
    selecting 92, 93
  in tasks view, changing width
    of 136
commands
  choosing 6
  hidden, displaying 7
Comment command 142
comments 141
completed tasks, recording 137, 141
Component/Banner Ad Manager
  command 120
Component/Hit Counter
  command 121
Component/Hover Button
  command 116
Component/Include Page
  command 144
Component/Marquee command 119
Component/Scheduled Include Page
  command 146
Component/Search Form
  command 102
Component/Substitution
  command 148
Component/Table of Contents
  command 122
contents
  decisions about 79
  frame, setting up 84
  tables of, adding to webs 122
Contents tab (Help window) 30
Control menu icon 31
copying text between webs 139
Corporate Presence Web
  Wizard 12
correcting misspellings 58
counting visitors 120, 121
Create A Page And Link To
  The New Page button 44

Index

Crop button 109
crop handles 109
cropping graphics 109
cropping tool 109
Custom.dic 61

D

data, collecting from forms 103
decisions
    audience 79
    content 79
    design 78
    graphics 80
Delete Cells button 91
Delete Cells command 91
Delete Cells command (shortcut menu) 97
Delete command (shortcut menu) 18, 73
deleting
    bookmarks 50
    cells 97
    columns from tables 91
    fields 97
    hyperlinks 66
    pages 17
        from published web 153
    rows from tables 91
    tables 91
    tasks 138
    webs 72
design decisions 78
designing for specific browsers 67
DHTML effects 114
    removing 115
DHTML Effects toolbar 114
dialog boxes, help with 29
dictionary, supplemental, adding words to 61
disabling ActiveX/Java 127
docking toolbars 8
documenting webs 141
download time, estimating 10
drag-and-drop editing in tables 92
drawing tables 90
Draw Table button 90
drop-down menu fields 97
Dynamic HyperText Markup Language. *See* DHTML

E

Edit Hyperlink command (shortcut menu) 65
Edit Task command (shortcut menu) 15, 138

editing
    drag-and-drop, in tables 92
    hotspots 114
    hyperlinks 65
    include pages 145
    placeholder forms 95
    tasks 138
    text 21
    undoing 17
    variables 149
e-mail hyperlinks 47
empty webs, creating 80
estimating download time 10
Exit command 31
expanded menus 7
expanding webs 16

F

favorites 50
feedback, tab-delimited 13
fields. *See* forms, fields
File command 22, 83
filenames, changing 28
files
    adding to webs 81
    associating with tasks 137
    creating tasks for 139
    inserting 22, 83
File Transfer Protocol (FTP) 70
flipping graphics 109
floating toolbars 8
folder list 12, 16
    turning on/off 16, 20, 28, 38, 63
Folder List button 16
folders
    adding to webs 81
    subweb 144
    view 16, 60
    web 10
Folders icon 16
font
    changing 25
    color of, changing 25
    size of, changing 25
Font box 25
Font Color button 25
Font command 25
Font Size box 25
formats
    graphic 38
    tab-delimited 13
formatting
    hover buttons 117
    navigation bars 53
    pages 24

    styles 24
    tables 93
Formatting toolbar 8
Form/Drop-Down Menu command 97
Form Field Properties command (shortcut menu) 98, 100
Form/Form command 96
Form/One-Line Text Box command 95
Form Page Wizard 96
Form Properties command (shortcut menu) 104
Form/Push Button command 100
Form/Radio Button command 97
forms 95
    adding to pages 96
    confirmation pages 100
    creating buttons on 100
    data collection 103
    editing placeholders 95
    fields 95
        deleting 97
        drop-down menus 97
        modifying 98
        one-line text box 95
        radio buttons 96
        scrolling text box 96
        validation rules for 101
    requiring entries 99
    tab order in 100
    testing 101
Frame Properties command 88
frames
    contents, setting up 84
    pages 82
        adding existing pages 86
        adding new pages 84
        hyperlinks in 87
        saving 85
        templates for 83
        testing 87, 88
        viewing in nonsupporting browsers 84
    size of, changing 88
Frames Page HTML tab (page view) 84
FrontPage
    concepts 10
    quitting 31
    running two instances of 139
    starting 5, 6
FrontPage Server Extensions 69, 95, 150

G

generating traffic 79
gif files 38
GIF Player 126
graphic
    formats 38
    hyperlinks 48
    keywords 39
graphics 108
    adding
        to hover buttons 116
        to pages 34
    adjusting brightness/contrast 108
    aligning
        absmiddle 39
        right 37
    animated 125
        previewing 126
    animating 114
    borders around 110
    cropping 109
    decisions about 80
    hotspots 111
        testing 113
    image maps 111
    importing 34
    inserting 111
    moving 36, 37, 40
    positioning 37
    properties of 37
    resampling 36
    restoring 110
    rotating/flipping 109
    saving as part of webs 38, 41
    scheduling 145
    searching for
        in Clip Art Gallery 39
        on Web 40
    selecting 36
    size of, changing 36, 37
    thumbnails 110
    using for hit counters 121
gridlines in tables, turning
    on/off 93

H

handles
    crop 109
    move 8
    selection 36
height of rows, changing 91
Help button (in dialog boxes) 29
Help feature 29
hidden
    commands, displaying 7
    toolbar buttons, displaying 9

hit counters 120
    using graphics 121
home page xii, 16
hotspots 111
    editing 114
    testing 113
    text 112
Hover Button Properties command
    (shortcut menu) 117
hover buttons 116
    adding graphics/sound to 116
    formatting 117
    testing 118
HTML xi, 4
    viewing tags 7, 24
HTML tab (page view) 24
Hyperlink button 44
Hyperlink command 47
hyperlinks xii, 10
    adding 43
        e-mail 47
        to existing pages 46
        to new pages 44
    to bookmarks 51
    buttons 21
    checking 62
    color of 45
    deleting 154
    displaying for pages 63
    editing 65
    e-mail 47
    to existing pages 87
    in frames pages 87
    graphic 48
    hotspots 111
    icons for 62
    to new pages 87, 151
    targets 43
    testing 46, 47, 87, 88
    text 43
    view 62
    to Web sites 48
Hyperlinks icon 62
HyperText Markup Language
    (HTML) xi, 4
    viewing tags 7, 24
HyperText Transfer Protocol (HTTP)
    44, 70

I

image maps 111
    testing 113
images. *See* graphics
Import command 81
importing
    graphics 34

include pages. *See* pages, include
Index tab (Help window) 30
initial capital letters 15
input forms. *See* forms
Insert/Caption command 94
Insert Clip button 35
Insert Columns button 91
inserting
    columns in tables 91
    files 22
    graphics 111
    include pages 144
    rows in tables 91, 93
    tables 90
    variables 147
Insert Rows button 91, 93
Insert/Rows Or Columns command 91
Insert Table button 90
Insert/Table command 90
International Cycling Union Web
    site 48
Internet xi
Internet Explorer 40, 67
Internet Service Providers
    (ISPs) 70
intranets xii

J

Java applets 126
    adding to pages 129
    disabling 127
joining cells 93
jpg files 38

K

keywords, graphic 39

L

labels (forms) 95
line breaks 26
links. *See* hyperlinks
List Properties command (shortcut
    menu) 28
lists
    bulleted 26
        changing bullet 28
    numbered 26

M

mailto hyperlinks 47
Make A Hyperlink That Sends E-mail
    button 47
maps, image 111
    testing 113
Mark As Completed command
    (shortcut menu) 137

Index

Marquee Properties command (shortcut menu) 119
marquees 118
menu bar 6
menus 6
   choosing commands 6
   displaying hidden commands 7
   expanding 7
   shortcut 7
Merge Cells button 93
merging cells 93
Microsoft FrontPage Help button 29
Microsoft FrontPage Server Extensions 69
Microsoft Internet Explorer. *See* Internet Explorer
Microsoft Office 4
Microsoft Web Publishing Wizard 71
Microsoft Web site 30
misspellings, correcting 58
modifying
   form fields 98
   themes 42
More Buttons button 9
Motion Clips tab (Clip Art Gallery) 35
move handle 8
moving
   columns in tables 92
   graphics 36, 37, 40
   pages 16, 19
   in tables 91
   toolbars 8
multiple frames on page 82

N

names
   of pages, changing 46
   vs. titles 19, 28
   of webs, specifying 80
navigation
   bars 21, 51
      adding 52
      organizing buttons on 53
      reformatting 53
      renaming buttons 54
      updating 52
   structure, updating 151
   view 15, 52, 151
      customizing 17
Navigation Bar command 52
Navigation Bar Properties command (shortcut menu) 53
Navigation icon 16
Navigation toolbar 16, 17
New Office Document command 6
New Page button 11, 18
New/Page command 18, 83
New/Task command 137
New/Web command 80
No Frames tab (page view) 84
Normal tab (page view) 23
numbered lists 26

O

objects, animated 114
one-line text box fields 95
Open button 27
Open File command (shortcut menu) 145
opening
   pages 27, 89
   second web 139
   webs 34, 89
Open Office Document command 6
Open Web command 89
organizing
   buttons on navigation bars 53
   webs 15, 80

P

page
   filenames, changing 28
   names, changing 46
   view 6, 20
      tabs 23
Page icon 6
Page Options command 67
Page Properties command (shortcut menu) 41, 123
pages xii, 10
   activating open 42
   adding 18
      ActiveX controls 127
      animated graphics 125
      banner ads 120
      forms 96
      graphics 34
      hyperlinks 43
      Java applets 129
      navigation bars 52
      plug-ins 130
      search capabilities 102
      sounds 123
      tables 90
      tables of contents 122
      time stamps 121
      to web structure 52
   applying themes 41
   background, changing 41
   blank, creating 143
   changing titles 86
   checking spelling of 59
   child 16
   confirmation (forms) 100
   deleting 17
   displaying hyperlinks for 63
   editing 21
   excluding from publication 153
   formatting 24
   frames 82
      adding existing pages 86
      adding new page 84
      hyperlinks in 87
      templates for 83
      testing 87, 88
      viewing in nonsupporting browsers 84
   home xii, 16
   hyperlinks to 44, 46, 87
   include 143
      editing 145
      inserting 144
      scheduled 145
   inserting files 83
   moving 16, 19
   moving to
      from tasks list 138
   names vs. titles 19, 28
   new
      blank 143
      hyperlinks to 151
      saving 46
   opening 27, 89
   parent 16
   peer 17, 21
   previewing 23, 53
   published, deleting 153
   publishing 150
      new/updated 152
   removing themes 42
   renaming 19, 86
   saving 81, 85
      new 46
   shared borders, turning on/off 54
   themes
      applying 41
      removing 42
      turning off 144
   using tables to control layout 94
paragraphs, space before 26
parent pages 16
peer pages 17, 21
picture bullets 28
Picture/Clip Art command 34, 39, 111
Picture/From File command 34

Picture Properties command (shortcut menu) 37, 109
pictures. See graphics
Pictures tab (Clip Art Gallery) 35
Pictures toolbar 108
Picture/Video command 125
placeholders
   forms, editing 95
   text 21, 22
Play Clip button 124
plug-ins 130
positioning
   graphics 36, 37
   tables 92
Preview In Browser button 67
previewing
   animated graphics 126
   pages 23, 53
   sounds 124
   webs 66
Preview tab (page view) 23, 67, 87, 88
Print button 68
Print command 68
printers, selecting 68
printing 68
priority of tasks, changing 138
proofreading 62, 68
published pages, deleting 153
publishing
   excluding pages from 153
   new/updated pages 150, 152
   webs 58, 69
Publish Web command 70, 71, 152

Q
quitting FrontPage 31

R
radio button fields 96
Refresh button 150
Refresh command 150
Remove Effect button 115
Rename command (shortcut menu) 19, 28
renaming
   files 28
   navigation bar buttons 54
   pages 19, 86
Reporting toolbar 65
Reports icon 64
Reports toolbar 64
reports view 63
Resample button 36

resampling graphics 36
Restore button 110
restoring graphics 110
Reveal Tags command 7
right-aligning
   table entries 93
   graphics 37
rotating graphics 109
rows in tables
   deleting 91
   height of, changing 91
   inserting 91, 93
   selecting 92

S
Save button 23
saving
   frames pages 85
   graphics as part of webs 38, 41
   pages 81, 85
      new 46
   sounds as part of webs 124
   webs 23
scheduled include pages 145
scheduling graphics 145
ScreenTips 8, 29
scrolling text box fields 96
search capabilities, adding to pages 102
searching
   for graphics
      in Clip Art Gallery 39
      on Web 40
   for Web site addresses 48, 70
second web, opening 139
Select/Column command 92
selecting
   columns in tables 92, 93
   graphics 36
   printers 68
   rows in tables 92
   tables 92
selection handles 36
Select/Row command 92
Select/Table command 92
servers, Web xii, 10
   addresses of 69
   sending webs to 71
Set Initial Page button 86
shared borders 26, 51
   displaying/hiding 54
   turning on/off 144
Shared Borders command 54
Shared Borders command (shortcut menu) 144
short menus 6

shortcut
   menus 7
   to FrontPage, creating on desktop 6
Show Task History command 138
sites, Web xi, 4, 10
   ActiveX 127
   addresses 44
      searching for 48, 70
   Clip Gallery Live 40
   generating traffic 79
   hyperlinks to 48
   International Cycling Union 48
   Java 129
   Microsoft 30
   Quick Course 49
   searching for addresses 48
   Yahoo 49
size
   of font 88
      changing 25
   of graphics, changing 36, 37
small capital letters 25
sorting tasks 137
sound effects 122
sounds
   adding to
      hover buttons 116
      pages 123
   previewing 124
   saving as part of webs 124
   testing 124
Sounds tab (Clip Art Gallery) 35
space before paragraphs 26
special effects 108
   DHTML effects 114
   hover buttons 116
   marquees 118
   sound 122
   video 124
spell checking 58
Spelling button 59
Standard toolbar 8
starting FrontPage 5, 6
Start Task command (shortcut menu) 15, 139, 142
status bar 6
styles, formatting with 24
style sheets, cascading 42
subwebs 144
superscripted text 25

T
tab-delimited formats 13
Table Properties command (shortcut menu) 92

Index

tables 89
  aligning 92
  borders around 93
  captions 93
  cells 91
    deleting 91, 97
    joining 93
  centering entries 93
  columns
    deleting 91
    inserting 91
    rearranging 92
    width of, changing 91
  of contents, adding to webs 122
  creating 90
  deleting 91
  drag-and-drop editing in 92
  drawing 90
  formatting 93
  gridlines, turning on/off 93
  moving around 91
  for page layout 94
  positioning 92
  right-aligning entries 93
  rows
    deleting 91
    height of, changing 91
    inserting 91, 93
  selecting 92
  titles, adding 92
tables of contents 122. *See also*
  contents frame
Table toolbar 92
tasks
  adding to list 135, 137
  assigning 140
  associating with files 137
  changing priority 138
  creating for other file types 139
  deleting 138
  editing 138
  list 134
    adding tasks 61
    jumping to page from 138
    widening columns 136
  recording as complete 137, 141
  sorting 137
  view 15, 135
    updating display 138
Tasks icon 15, 135
templates for frames pages 83
testing
  forms 101
  frames pages 87, 88
  hotspots 113
  hover buttons 118

  hyperlinks 46, 47
  sounds 124
  webs 72
text
  aligning 26
  blinking 25
  centering 26
  copying between webs 139
  editing 21
  hotspots 112
  hyperlinks 43
  in marquees 118
  placeholders 21, 22
  superscripted 25
Theme command 42
Theme command (shortcut menu)
  42, 144
themes 41
  modifying 42
  removing from pages 42
  turning off 144
thumbnail graphics 110
time stamps 121
title bar 6
titles
  adding to tables 92
  vs. names 19, 28
  of pages, changing 86
toolbar row 9
toolbars 8
  displaying hidden buttons 9
  turning on/off 16

U

Undo button 17
undoing editing 17
Universal Resource Locators (URLs)
  xi, 44
updating
  navigation structure 151
  tasks view display 138
  variables 149
  Web sites 150
up-to-date webs, maintaining 141
URLs xi, 44
Use Your Web Browser To Select A
  Page Or File button 49

V

validation rules in form fields 101
variables 147
  creating 149
  editing 149
  inserting 147
Verify Hyperlinks button 64
video effects 124

viewing
  folder list 16, 60
  HTML tags 7, 24
  hyperlinks 62
  pages 6, 20
  tasks 15, 135
  web structure 15, 52, 151
views
  folders 16, 60
  hyperlinks 62
  navigation 15, 52, 151
    customizing 17
  page 6, 20
    tabs 23
  reports 63
  switching 20
  tasks 15, 135
Views bar 6
  Folders icon 16
  Hyperlinks icon 62
  Navigation icon 16
  Page icon 6
  Reports icon 64
  Tasks icon 15, 135

W

Web xi, 4
  browsers xii
    designing for 67
  servers xi, xii, 10
    addresses of 69
    sending webs to 71
  sites xi, 4, 10
    ActiveX 127
    addresses 44, 48, 70
    Clip Gallery Live 40
    generating traffic 79
    hyperlinks to 48
    International Cycling Union 48
    Java 128
    Microsoft 30
    Quick Course 49
    searching for addresses 48
    updating 150
    Yahoo 49
web information 147
Web pages. *See* pages
Web Presence Providers (WPPs) 70
Web Settings command 149
webs 10
  adding
    files/folders 81
    new to existing 80
  checking spelling of 60
  closing 89
  collapsing/expanding 16

confirmation pages 100
copying
   text between 139
creating 10
   from scratch 78, 80
   using wizard 11
deleting 72
documenting 141
folders for 10
frames pages 82
   adding existing pages 86
   adding pages 84
   hyperlinks in 87
   saving 85
   templates for 83
   testing 87, 88
   viewing in nonsupporting
      browsers 84
inserting
   files 22
keeping up to date 141
naming folders 80
opening 34, 89
   second 139
organizing 15, 80
pages
   activating open 42
   adding 18
   adding to structure 52
   ActiveX controls in 127
   animated graphics in 125
   applying themes 41
   background, changing 41
   banner ads in 120
   blank, creating 143

   changing titles 86
   checking spelling of 59
   child 16
   confirmation 100
   controlling layout with
      tables 94
   creating blank 143
   deleting 17
   editing 21
   excluding from publication 153
   formatting 24
   forms in 96
   graphics in 34
   home 16
   hyperlinks in 43
   hyperlinks to 44, 46
   include 143
   inserting files 83
   Java applets in 129
   moving 16, 19
   names vs. titles 19, 28
   navigation bars in 52
   opening 27, 89
   parent/child 16
   peer 17
   plug-ins in 130
   previewing 23
   removing themes 42
   renaming 19, 86
   saving 81
   saving new 46
   scheduled include 145
   search capabilities in 102
   shared borders, turning
      on/off 54

   sounds in 123
   tables of contents in 122
   time stamps in 121
   turning off themes 144
   planning 11
   previewing 66
   printing 68
   publishing 58, 69
      updated 150, 152
   saving 23
   sending to Web servers 71
   spell-checking 58
   subwebs 144
   testing 72
width of columns, changing
   in tables 91
   in tasks view 136
Windows 5
wizards
   Answer 30
   Corporate Presence Web 12
   creating webs with 11
   Form Page 96
   Microsoft Web Publishing 71
words
   adding to supplemental
      dictionary 61
   checking spelling of 58
World Wide Web. *See* Web
WPPs 70

Y

Yahoo 49

Quick Course® Books

Offering beginning to intermediate training, Quick Course® books are updated regularly. For information about the most recent titles, call 1-800-854-3344 or e-mail us at quickcourse@otsiweb.com.

AVAILABLE QUICK COURSE®BOOKS		
1-58278-005-6	Quick Course® in Microsoft Access 2000	$14.95
1-879399-73-3	Quick Course® in Microsoft Access 97	$14.95
1-879399-52-0	Quick Course® in Microsoft Access 7	$14.95
1-879399-32-6	Quick Course® in Access 2	$14.95
1-58278-003-X	Quick Course® in Microsoft Excel 2000	$14.95
1-879399-71-7	Quick Course® in Microsoft Excel 97	$14.95
1-879399-51-2	Quick Course® in Microsoft Excel 7	$14.95
1-879399-28-8	Quick Course® in Excel 5	$14.95
1-58278-008-0	Quick Course® in Microsoft FrontPage 2000	$14.95
1-879399-91-1	Quick Course® in the Internet Using Microsoft Internet Explorer 5	$14.95
1-879399-68-7	Quick Course® in Microsoft Internet Explorer 4	$14.95
1-879399-67-9	Quick Course® in the Internet Using Netscape Navigator, ver. 2 & 3	$14.95
1-58278-001-3	Quick Course® in Microsoft Office 2000	$24.95
1-879399-69-5	Quick Course® in Microsoft Office 97	$24.95
1-879399-54-7	Quick Course® in Microsoft Office for Windows 95/NT	$24.95
1-879399-39-3	Quick Course® in Microsoft Office for Windows, ver. 4.3	$24.95
1-58278-006-4	Quick Course® in Microsoft Outlook 2000	$14.95
1-879399-80-6	Quick Course® in Microsoft Outlook 98	$14.95
1-58278-004-8	Quick Course® in Microsoft PowerPoint 2000	$14.95
1-879399-72-5	Quick Course® in Microsoft PowerPoint 97	$14.95
1-879399-33-4	Quick Course® in PowerPoint 4	$14.95
1-58278-007-2	Quick Course® in Microsoft Publisher 2000	$14.95
1-58278-000-5	Quick Course® in Microsoft Windows 2000	$15.95
1-879399-81-4	Quick Course® in Microsoft Windows 98	$15.95
1-879399-34-2	Quick Course® in Windows 95	$14.95
1-879399-14-8	Quick Course® in Windows 3.1	$14.95
1-879399-22-9	Quick Course® in Windows for Workgroups	$14.95
1-879399-64-4	Quick Course® in Windows NT Workstation 4	$16.95

AVAILABLE QUICK COURSE®BOOKS		
1-58278-002-1	Quick Course® in Microsoft Word 2000	$14.95
1-879399-70-9	Quick Course® in Microsoft Word 97	$14.95
1-879399-50-4	Quick Course® in Microsoft Word 7	$14.95
1-879399-27-X	Quick Course® in Word 6	$14.95
1-879399-49-0	Quick Course® in WordPerfect 6.1 for Windows	$14.95

Volume discounts available for orders of 5 or more of the same title.

Quick Course® Workbooks

Providing additional practice exercises and true/false and fill-in-the-blank quizzes, the workbooks are sold only with an accompanying Quick Course® book and in quantities of FIVE or more. Exercise and answer files are provided in an Instructor's Resource packet, which is free with orders of TEN or more workbooks.

AVAILABLE WORKBOOKS		
1-879399-78-4	Microsoft Access 97 Workbook	$11.95
1-879399-84-9	Access 97 Instructor's Resource Packet	$11.95
1-879399-77-6	Microsoft Excel 97 Workbook	$11.95
1-879399-85-7	Excel 97 Instructor's Resource Packet	$11.95
1-58278-010-2	Microsoft Office 2000 Workbook	$14.95
1-58278-014-5	Office 2000 Instructor's Resource Packet	$14.95
1-879399-74-1	Microsoft Office 97 Workbook	$14.95
1-879399-83-0	Office 97 Instructor's Resource Packet	$14.95
1-879399-65-2	Microsoft Office 95 Workbook	$14.95
1-879399-66-0	Office 95 Instructor's Resource Packet	$14.95
1-879399-46-6	Microsoft Office ver. 4.3 Workbook	$14.95
1-879399-45-8	Office 4.3 Instructor's Resource Packet	$14.95
1-879399-79-2	Microsoft PowerPoint 97 Workbook	$11.95
1-879399-86-5	PowerPoint 97 Instructor's Resource Packet	$11.95
1-879399-76-8	Microsoft Word 97 Workbook	$11.95
1-879399-87-3	Word 97 Instructor's Resource Packet	$11.95
1-879399-88-1	Microsoft Windows 98 Workbook	$12.75
1-879399-89-X	Windows 98 Instructor's Resource Packet	$12.75

Prices and availability are subject to change without notice.

Quick Course® Online Training

For those times when books alone don't quite fit the bill, Quick Course® training is now offered online.

This exciting new CD-ROM-based, interactive option incorporates video demonstrations into the acclaimed Quick Course® hands-on training format. Each title is fully searchable and includes a detailed table of contents and a comprehensive index. Document files are provided for each unit so that tasks can be tackled in the order presented in the course or on an as-needed basis. Web-based support is provided for all online courses.

Quick Course® online training can be delivered via CD-ROM, the Internet, or an intranet. It is ideal for self-paced training and can facilitate and enhance instructor-led courses. Titles are sold as individual copies or as site licenses. Please call for pricing information.

AVAILABLE IN ONLINE FORMAT
Quick Course® in Microsoft Access 2000
Quick Course® in Microsoft Excel 2000
Quick Course® in Microsoft FrontPage 2000
Quick Course® in Microsoft Office 2000
Quick Course® in Microsoft PowerPoint 2000
Quick Course® in Microsoft Publisher 2000
Quick Course® in Microsoft Word 2000